STEREOTYPES IN ORGANIZATIONS: A STUDY OF AFRICAN AMERICAN

WOMEN IN ORGANIZATIONAL LEADERSHIP

AND THE GLASS CEILING

STEREOTYPES IN ORGANIZATIONS: A STUDY OF

AFRICAN AMERICAN WOMEN IN ORGANIZATIONAL

LEADERSHIP

AND THE GLASS CEILING

ABSTRACT

Inquiry implies that although women have evolved in their depiction in organizational and leadership management positions and roles, especially in three different North Carolina State governmental agencies, they are still subject to gender inequality (Cohen & Huffman, 2003; Gazso, 2004;). For African American women, they are further imperiled to race and class inequalities. The purported research is envisioned to investigate and distinguish the distinctive individual and professional interpretations and occurrences of 18 African American women that are in managerial or leadership roles in North Carolina state government working in a White, male-dominated culture. The study will broaden and engage conversations about gender inequality and ascertain whether these African American, working in such an environment and culture, agree in their perceptions of inequalities and how it correlates to the low representation in managerial and leadership positions within their respective organizations.

2

ACKNOWLEDGEMENTS

I first give all the glory, honor and praise to Jesus Christ, my Lord and Savior. Without him, I would be nothing. To my mother, Elizabeth W. Montague, my rock and source of inspiration, I know you're watching me from heaven. Your belief in me continues to cheer me and you know my pain and struggles through this process. To my wonderful Papi, the Rev. Nathaniel Montague, I love you and thank you for the encouragement and support, and now I can get out of your pockets (smile). To my Aunt Myrtle Strickland-Shepard, thank you, thank you, and thank you. To my mother from another mother/auntie, Andrea Jones, thank you for being there for me; you are a constant support in all that I do. To my brother and sister-in-law and friends, Paul Jones and Keisha Jacobs-Jones, you guys rock! We've gone through a lot of tears and laughs together throughout the years, and I appreciate all you have done for me and continue to do. Love you guys! To Kimberly Khan and Shannon Reid, my partners in crime; words cannot even explain how much I appreciate you all. To Jae Williams, you said I could do it. I thank you for your strength and words of encouragement through the rough and rocky times. To anyone I have missed, please don't blame my heart but my mind. To those who also have given me courage and I have forgotten to mention here, thank you as well. Finally, to Dr. B., thank you for your patience, above any and everything else. It has been a long journey, but you were able to keep me intact and somewhat sane through this process, and I commend you and thank you.

DEDICATION

This is dedicated to my mother, the late Elizabeth W. Montague; all those who believed and encouraged me; and to Zeta Phi Beta Sorority, Inc. for helping me become the woman I am today.

LIST OF TABLES

6

TABLE OF CONTENTS

CHAPTER ONE: INTRODUCTION

What does it take to be a leader? Is it looks, wealth, power, charisma or all of the above? According to Jago (1982,) "Good leaders are made not born. If you have the determination and drive, you can become a successful leader (p.318). Good leaders progress throughout a continuous development of identity, analysis, learning, preparation and knowledge.

Leadership can be described as a process by which a person influences others to accomplish an objective and directs the organization in a way that makes it more cohesive and coherent (Northouse (2007, p.3) defines leadership as a process whereby an individual influences a group of individuals to achieve a common goal. Leaders can convey the leadership process by employing their immediate leadership skills, knowledge and abilities, better known as Process Leadership (Jago, 1982). African American women have contributed and made significant contributions to the workforce throughput the years. However, there is little research that focuses on professional leadership roles of women of color in the workplace (Burke, 2003). America is known for producing an essence of ingenuity, and African American women have been major contributors as groundbreaking leaders of inventiveness. Madame Noire (2012) suggests "the resourcefulness of women who rose from the ashes of slavery to the brilliant creativity of modern day geniuses, our lives are immeasurably better, due to black women's contributions to America" :(para. 6). African American women of note include Marie Van Brittan Brown, born in 1922, who was the first person to develop the patent for closed circuit television security; and Dr. Shirley Jackson, the first female black to receive a doctorate from the Massachusetts Institute of Technology (MIT) as well as the first black female to become president of a major technological institute, Rensselaer Polytechnic Institute. However, we do not hear of these women's accomplishments in mainstream media or see reference to them in schools history lessons, not even during Black History Month.

With the election of President Obama, more discussion has taken place in organizations of how the election of the first African American President will influence opportunities for minorities, especially African American women, to move into executive positions of leadership (Collins, 2009). In order to evaluate such prospects, The Executive Leadership Council (ELC) ordered a poll of 150 executives soon after the election. The ELC is a national organization that consists of current and former African American Chief Executive Officers (CEOs) and senior executives at Fortune 500 and equivalent companies that have been operating for more than 25 years. The poll found that 75 percent of the executives surveyed thought that permitting minorities in senior executive and leadership roles is especially imperative to presenting new ideas and better reflect the diversity of clienteles (Collins, 2009). Unfortunately, this perspective demonstrated that African American women faced serious trials climbing the corporate ladder. Thirty-one percent of surveyed executives ascribed those challenges to weaker or less planned associations available to African American women. According to Collins (2009),"Inaccurate perceptions of African American women's capabilities (24 percent) and work/life balance demands (23 percent) round out the top three issues cited as preventing or slowing down their rise."

Statement of the Problem

The subject of leadership has been studied in multiple facets varying from development of styles to motivational influences. Feminist epistemology has been described as the examination of how gender manipulates one's perception of lived experiences (Anderson,

2004). Certain theories, such as the Feminist Standpoint Theory, emphasize gender relations and the role of research as an influence for social change (Anderson, 2004). Womanist doctrine can be described as the image upon the African American woman's place in society (Thomas, 2000). Womanism has also been described as the integration of ethnic and feminist consciousness among women of color (King, 2003).

Despite the research efforts of feminists, womanist theologians and theorists, an increasingly more diverse workforce continues to be an issue with an inadequate representation of African American women in management and leadership roles and positions in organizations, especially in the area of organizational leadership in a world of White, male-dominated cultures. However, when African American women are placed into positions and roles of leadership, retaining women of color becomes a problem due to the fact that these women are constantly battling inequalities such as gender variations in pay, job isolation and discrimination (Giscombe & Mattis, 2002; Mitra, 2003). Patricia L. Charlemagne, Chief Operating Officer of Future Leaders Institute Charter School, concurs that African American women strive to be embraced in vital networks. Charlemagne (Collins, 2009) further states, "In the workplace, people develop and form relationship based on commonalities and thus where there are a limited number of black female executives, it is easier to remain an outsider."

The Bureau of Labor Statistics Census (2002 & 2010) conducted a nationwide study that assessed the wages of men and women of all races and ethnicities. This study showed inequities, given that African American women with bachelor's degrees or advanced degrees grossed less than White women. The 2002 census found that 26 percent of African American women were in leadership and managerial roles, and 37 percent of White women held those same positions. The researcher received approval to conduct the study with the public sectors of three organizations in Raleigh, North Carolina, whereby the public sector consists of the Office of the State Controller (OSC), Department of Public Safety (DPS), and the Department of Health and Human Services (DHHS). The study featured 18 African American women in leadership roles among the three organizations.

Background of the Problem

The précis of African American women has transformed radically over the past six decades, according to Parker (2003). Parker (2003) also states, "In 1949, 42 percent of African American female

14

employees worked in domestic service." "In the United States (1990), 19 percent were in managerial and professional occupations, and 39 percent were in technical or administrative positions" (O'Hare, Pollard, Mann, & Kent, 1992). Even with the rise of African American women placed into positions and roles of power within organizations and institutions of higher learning, their ability to become and remain effective organizational leaders is questioned. Osuoha (2010) stated, "Although most companies consider their diversity plan initiatives to be a successful part of promoting inclusiveness, 66% of African Americans surveyed believe that these programs do not address the issue of racism that continues to exist against their racial group." Osuoha (2010) further stated that "In addition, most women surveyed believe that their opportunities for job advancements are declining over time (Catalyst, 2004a)."

Smith (2008) stated that asserted African American women have generate alternative practices and knowledge tied to their lived experiences that are designed to foster empowerment and better those experiences (Collins, 2000). Smith (2008) further stated, "African American women not only experience gender bias that stems from the false premise that males are better suited to hold leadership positions

(Bell & Chase, 1993; Coleman, 2005), but are also confronted by racial bias (Valverde, 2003) historically embedded in the power structures of organizations and African American women find themselves in a position of "double jeopardy" since either their gender or race may evoke negative responses from employers (Dardaine- Raggeut, 1994; Doughty, 1980)."

Purpose of the Study

The purpose of this study was to describe the trials and tribulations of 18 African American women in leadership roles in the public sector and explore the employment experiences of this diverse group of proficient and qualified women in the workplace as they bid to escalate into their prospective management and leadership roles not only in corporate America, but in governmental entities as well. This analysis focused on individual personal motivations, morals, success factors, barriers such as race, diversity issues, gender differences and leadership capabilities and practices and the impact that these items has on the women.

Research Questions

The research questions are as follows:

1. What are the leadership characteristics of African American women serving in leadership roles, such as in upper management in organizations?

2. Is there a significant difference in the leadership behavior and style of African American women leaders versus White, Hispanic and Asian women and White, Hispanic and Asian males and what are the differences if any?

3. Do you believe there is a correlation between the educational levels of African American women employees who advance to the highest positions in the workplace in the United States and the African American women who do not receive advancements? If yes, what type of relationship levels exist?

4. Does economic and social background, such as coming from a poor, middle or upper class upbringing, play a deciding factor in an African American woman's ability to obtain a leadership role in an organization and could you explain in detail the reason for your response?

Limitations and Delimitations

This study undertakes that the participants of the research would respond to interview questions honorably and straightforwardly, and provide answers with sincerity. This study is intended to comprehend the trials, tribulations and overall experiences of African American women working in leadership roles in public organizations. This study was limited, due to the sample population being 18 African American women who have leadership roles either as managers or directors in a public or private entity. Unambiguously, the sample population was not illustrative of African American women beyond 18 participants. Participants for the research were chosen from three separate North Carolina governmental state agencies. The first state agency employs 200 hundred people, and three participants are from this agency. The second state agency employs 4,000 people, and 10 participants are from this agency; and the third state agency employs 19,210 individuals, and 5 individuals are participants. This study does not discuss experiences of leadership of the African American woman in the structure of a female controlled organization.

Definitions

African American Women: Women whose origin is from the black racial groups. It is synonymous with black women and is used interchangeably.

Discrimination: Discrimination refers to distinguishable treatment of an individual or group of individuals based on prejudicial treatment.

Women of Color: Non-white women, i.e. black women, Hispanics, Asian Americans and Native Americans.

Glass Ceiling: Glass ceiling refers to the barriers, based on unfairness in an organization and or a division within the organization, that prevents qualified applicants or individuals from advancing in their organization in a leadership/managerial position based on specific gender or racial inequality.

White Women: Women of non-color that derives from European ancestry.

Importance of the Study

The purpose of this study was to evaluate and review the trials and tribulations of African American women in leadership roles in the public sector and explore the employment experiences of this diverse group of proficient and qualified women in the workplace as the women bid to escalate into their prospective management and leadership roles in governmental entities, and to identify whether these women are experiencing the "glass ceiling" syndrome. Results of this study on African American women and their occupational voyage to become leaders in the workplace is extremely important because the study can construct a speculative structure in which organizations, whether it be in the private or public sector can develop and/or improve equitable policies, pay, procedures, and practices. This study will broaden consciousness, concerning equal hiring and promotional practices in addition to functioning as an additional resource in organizational leadership and management structure development within organizational cultures. Understanding unique perceived discriminatory barriers and addressing issues such as the concerns of African American women will bring awareness of how job performance and job satisfaction can be improved, therefore, providing more opportunities for advancement for African American women. Johnson (2005) pointed out that Higginbotham contended that because there is a limited amount of women of color in corporate positions, more detailed investigations should be done so that we will know more about the psychology of African American women and what they experience in the workplace (p. 8).

Nature of the Study

A qualitative method using a combination of grounded theory was used to conduct this study that enabled the researcher to have the chance to use real life situations and experiences of study participants. Interviews were conducted using a voice recorder to document the responses to the interview questions, along with notes taken while the interview is being conducted.

The purpose of this research was to study to focus on 18 African American women from the public sector in North Carolina state government who are managers and leaders within their prospective organizations and understand how they felt about barriers and investigated causes that influenced the small number of African American leaders in their organizations. Another purpose of this study was to apprehend how the existing realisms relate to workplace disparities and the connections of gender, race, social-economic background and education for the 18 African American women.

Anticipated Findings

The discernment of why there is a lack of African American women employed in executive and leadership positions within a society that is controlled and dominated by White males is grounded on a belief of inequitableness and injustice that leaders center their choices on inapt influences and not implementation. The perception of irrelevant factors and not implementation, have ruled development prospects for African American women for years. A majority of individuals with acquired and demonstrated talent in the workplace want an unbiased opportunity to have a say and make a difference within the organization.

CHAPTER TWO: REVIEW OF THE LITERATURE

Introduction

This chapter reviews the literature pertaining to African American women in managerial and leadership roles, with emphasis African American women facing challenges in a White, male dominated business society. Women are described as using leadership qualities derived from their own multifaceted societal and cultural accounts (Ah Nee Benham & Cooper, 1998). The gender structure in the traditional home and the educational setting is based on a dominant male whose authority is unquestioned according to Miller, Washington, and Fiene (2006). Butler and Skattebo (2004) proved that society has stereotyped individuals by gender. Even though these matters are continuously studied, there is a break in the research amongst the chance for and depiction of African American women managers and leaders that are employed in a White, male dominated organization regardless if it is in corporate America or within the public sector. Women often face discrimination in the workplace in general. However, it has been noted that African American women faces the most discrimination in the workplace. The African American woman is viewed through lens colored by gender and racial bias as well as societal and cultural expectations and stereotypes (Rusher, 1996). The lesser wages of African American female managers could relatively be accredited to the circumstance that they are isolated in primarily female occupations, such Administrative Assistants or Executive Assistants (Johnson, 2010). Furthermore, in contrast to African American males and white females, African American females do not earn significant wage premiums associated with supervisory duties. This trend has also been exhibited in school administrative roles, where there are not enough African American women in school administration (Emerald insight, 2004). The role of both entrepreneurial and business women is considered today as an important source of economic growth, employment and innovation (Coleman, 2000). Twenty years ago, analysts and researchers acknowledged comparisons in the educational background between men and women. Yet, these analysts and researchers identified the "glass ceiling" effect taking place throughout organizations, regardless of private or public organizations and this type of effect made it challenging for women in the workplace. At the start of the 21st century, Leonard (2001) evaluated women's circumstances in the workplace, concluding that no significant changes had been made from the decade before regarding gender and race

24

inequalities and discrimination. The first section of this chapter will

focus on the glass ceiling syndrome and what this syndrome, means.

The second section of this chapter will focus on the underrepresentation

of African Americans and racism in management and the third section

will focus on discrimination of women in the workplace and how

discrimination has made it difficult for women, especially African

American women to obtain leadership roles. The fourth and fifth

sections will discuss societal and cultural female functions,

characterizations and expectations, and institutional and organizational

barriers, respectively.

Glass Ceiling Syndrome

The information given here discusses the difficulties of

prejudice that have apprehended women from succeeding into

leadership roles. The term glass ceiling was established by Hymowitz

and Schellhardt in 1986, based on a Wall Street Journal article that

focused on the difficulties and barriers women encountered as they

made efforts to advance on the corporate ladder. The term "Glass

ceiling" also suggests the unseen mock obstacles produced by

preconceptions that keep women from managerial positions (Elmuti, et

al., 2003). Since the publication of the Wall Street Journal article on the glass ceiling, the definition of the glass ceiling has included minorities, particularly women of color. The article also caused the government to establish the Federal Glass Commission in 1992; the purpose of the commission is to establish and identify rules and regulations for inequalities and recognize hindrances that have obstructed the progression of minorities and females. The Federal Glass Commission also identified issues such as race, gender, stereotypes, education, as well as nepotism that hindered women and minorities from advancing into leadership and managerial roles in the private sector. Johnson (2010) stated, "The term Glass ceiling was first used by the National Commission on Glass Ceilings in 1991." The phrase "glass ceiling" describes what happened to women and minorities when they were denied the opportunity to advance to upper levels of executive management because of gender or race (Baxter, Wright & Birkelund, 2000)."

Individuals of color or women of color face barriers that are difficult to cross. The Department of Labor identified and publicized the glass ceiling problem and issued a report on the Glass Ceiling project along with the introduction of the Glass Ceiling Act in 1991, which became known as Title Il of the Civil Rights Act of 1991

(Federal Glass Ceiling Commission, 1995). The Federal government's motivation for conducting the study was due to Hymowitz and Schellhardt's 1986 study's findings that African American women and Latinas were not being given the same opportunities in the workplace as men and white women. Johnson (2010) revealed "The Federal Glass Ceiling Commission (1995) established three levels of artificial barriers to the development of women and minorities which were identified as a result of the study." The three levels were:

1. Societal obstacles, which may be external to the direct jurisdiction of the establishment.

2. Resource difficulties as they convey to educational opportunity, achievement and persons being equipped to go into higher levels of management.

3. Dissimilarity impediments as demonstrated in conscious and unconscious stereotyping, prejudices and biases related to gender, race and ethnicity. (pp. 7-8)

According to Johnson (2010) the investigation also assessed institutional or in-house hurdles that are within the direct control of organizations. The institutional barriers included:

1. Outreach and enlistment methods that do not pursue to reach or enlist minorities and women

2. Internal atmospheres that disaffect and segregate minorities and women

3. Pipeline obstacles that straightforwardly disturb chances for progression

4. Preliminary assignment and assembling in workforce jobs or in favorably methodological and professional trades that is not on the professional road to the top

5. Absence of mentoring

6. Nonexistence of management training

7. Absence of chance for career development

8. Slight or no access to critical developmental assignments such as memberships greatly noticeable task forces and committees

9. Distinctive or unusual standards for performance evaluation

10. Trivial or no access to informal networks of communication.

(Federal Glass Ceiling Commission 1995, p. 8)

Governmental or political barriers, according to the study, were identified as (Johnson, 2010):

1. Absence of exuberant, coherent monitoring of establishment employment practices.

2. Limitations in the collection and disaggregating of employment related data, making it difficult to ascertain the status of groups at the managerial level.

3. Insufficient recording and dissemination of information relevant to glass ceiling issues. (Federal Glass Ceiling Commission 1995, p. 8)

All of the barriers that were acknowledged as causative to the inequalities of the number of women as well as the minorities who reach prime decision-making and or policy-making positions in the workplace seem to raise questions and concerns. The research also revealed that women and minorities that were in higher level positions, such as leadership roles, were compensated lower than their male counterparts. The occurrence of any type of ceiling which proposes or creates barriers to the higher level of managerial positions and disparities in salaries creates a gender gap in authority (Baxter et al., 2000).

According to Ovadia & Vannerman (2001), "Not all gender or racial inequalities can be defined as glass ceilings." Ovadia & Vannerman's (2001) definition of the glass ceiling is a particular kind of racial or gender bias that is distinguishable from other types of inequities regarding race or gender. According to Cotter et al., these glass-ceiling barriers form a deep line of demarcation between those who prosper and those left behind. Their description of the glass ceiling is a definition which refrain women and minorities from advancing up the corporate ladder, specifically in managerial and leadership roles, regardless of their education, social status, knowledge and abilities to perform the particular job. Cotter et al. identified four criteria that identify glass-ceiling effects versus job place inequalities (2001). The first criterion suggests that the true existence of a glass ceiling must validate job discrimination that is unexplained by a person's past qualifications or achievements. Criterion two indicates that a glass ceiling represents a gender or racial difference that is greater at higher levels than at lower levels of employment within the company (Cotter, et al. 2001). In criterion three, a glass ceiling is present when there is discrimination in opportunity for advancement, promotions and salary increases. Criterion four implies that a ceiling exists if some upward movement has been made in the past but later in one's career more severe discrimination sets in to block further progress (Cotter, et al., 2001).

Governmental agencies and entities on the local, state and federal levels have established their own policies and procedures on unfair hiring and promotional practices in conjuncture with the Federal Glass Commission's regulations. States such as North Carolina has the Office of State Personnel (OSP) to establish hiring and promotional practices for their state agencies, which is to ensure all employees - no matter the race, creed, nationality, gender or sex - is treated fair and all are given the same advancement opportunities. However, the glass ceiling syndrome still prevails in many instances. The federal equal employment opportunity laws prohibiting job discrimination are (Grin, 2006):

Title VII of the Civil Rights Act of 1964 (Title VII), which prohibits employment discrimination based on race, color, religion, sex, or national origin; the Equal Pay Act of 1963 (EPA), which protects men and women who perform substantially equal work in the same establishment from sex-based wage discrimination; the Age Discrimination in Employment Act of 1967 (ADEA), which protects individuals who are 40 years of age or older; Title I and Title V of the Americans with Disabilities Act of 1990 (ADA), which prohibit employment discrimination against qualified individuals with disabilities in private sector, and in state and local governments; Sections 501 and 505 of the Rehabilitation Act of 1973, which prohibit discrimination against qualified individuals with disabilities who work in the federal government; and the Civil Rights Act of 1991, which, among other things, provides monetary damages in cases of intentional employment discrimination (U.S. Environmental Protection Agency, n.d., para. 4) .

Even though females have attained more prominence in organizations than the last century, opportunities for advancement or salaries comparable to men who hold the same positions are still not obtainable (Grin, 2006). In 2004, Catalyst conducted a study that established that diversity has a progressive impact on financial performance and companies that had the top representation of women in leadership and managerial roles had a better performance in regards to financial performance compared to organizations that had a low representation of women in in leadership roles. Companies that enlist, keep, train and give the knowledge and abilities to develop women's skills are more viable universally in the workplace. According to Grin (2006), "The sample for this study included a review of the financial performance of companies that won the Catalyst Award between 1996 and 2003." Osuoha (2010) also stated, "Women in key managerial positions are increasing very slowly as women chair only 11.2% of the board of directors of the Fortune 500 companies sampled." In 2006, Grin researched that advancing women up as a business approach is profitable; however, women seem to encounter problems of gender bias and glass ceilings (Claes, 1999). "Women also continue to come in and out of the workplace as caregivers to children and elderly parents" (J. Collins, 2004; Kirchmeyer, 2002). Also it was suggested "women still dawdle after men in opportunity and recompense" (Brett & Stroh, 1999). Women and minorities are no longer considered just as individuals employed in the labor force. Patterson (2006) notes that their successes and contributions to the economy should not and cannot go unrecognized. Unfortunately women, especially African American women, do not get the recognition that is deserved.

Leadership Theory

Leadership theories have been categorized into a few categories which include: behavioral, situational, contingency, transformational and transactional theories. Behavioral theory undertakes that leaders are made and not born. Behavioral theory observes what the leader does as well as examines leader development and organizational success (Argyris, 2000). Situation theory exists when certain leaders' behaviors and situations is more effective than other theories (Bess & Goldman, 2001). Johnson (2010) states, "Contingency theory assumes that a leader's ability to lead is reliant upon circumstantial factors" (Casmir, 2001; Lowe & Gardner, 2000). Trait theory dons the view that individuals are born with innate characteristics predominantly coordinated to leadership (Bess & Goldman, 2001; Lowe & Gardner, 2000). Transformational theory constructs the assumptions about empowerment and that people will abide by individuals who can inspire zeal and energize others (Bess & Goldman, 2001; Cacoullos, 2001; Casmir, 2001; Eagly & Johannesen-Schmidt, 2001; Yoder, 2001). Transactional theory is based on the premise that punishment and rewarding those that deserve some type of compensation for the

34

good work and or deed that they have exhibited and rewards is the main motivator for this theory (Conger & Kanungo, 1994; Bass, 1985).

Feminist Standpoint Theory

Anderson's (2004) feminist standpoint theory stresses gender relations and the role of research as an influence for social change (p.25). The feminist standpoint theory stems from the Marxist view, which asserts an epistemic opportunity over fundamental questions, history and sociology. Those that are socially oppressed will not be able to obtain information and understanding that is only available to the socially advantaged, especially knowledge of social relations and this theory concentrates further on the political aspect of the standpoint - a feminist standpoint and not a woman's standpoint (Johnson, 2010), which has attempted to add to the diversity of women and the standpoints of other marginalized groups (Anderson, 2004). The intentions of the feminist standpoint theory are parallel to the social world in relation to the welfare of the subjects under analysis, provide criticism whether it be constructive or not to the subjects of study in order to develop their perception of their nuisances, and to propose the techniques to correct disparities. In 2001, Harding indicated that standpoint theorists now focus on the value of inferior people versus adamant claims regarding group differences (Johnson, 2010).

Underrepresentation in Management and Racism

Cohen and Huffman (2007) notes that "inequality is a major contributor to the underrepresentation of African Americans in management and leadership roles in organizations regardless of the private or public sectors" (para. 8). The two researchers also believed that there is a population proportion, black to white inequality that is causing the disparity of lack of African Americans in management especially African American women and also formulated a visibility-discrimination hypothesis. The University of North Carolina-Chapel Hill (2007) reported, "This visibility-discrimination hypothesis ascribes a positive association amongst racial attentiveness and inequality to a white response to the threat posed by larger minority group size (Blalock 1967; Burr, Galle, and Fossett 1991; Beggs, Villemez, and Arnold 1997)." Also according to the University of North Carolina-Chapel Hill (2007), Glenn (1963) stated, "Whites have more to gain from discriminating in areas with a higher percentage of blacks." The investigation conducted on this hypothesis also focused on the actions and outlooks of whites, which validates the hypothesis (Burr, Galle, and Fossett 1991). The relationship between African Americans and whites' anti-black actions has been historically shown through lynching and racial riots that were happening in the Deep South in the 50s and 60s.

Based on Cohen and Huffman's (2007) research and findings, they stated "These studies complement research showing a positive relationship between percentage black in the local population and whites' anti-black attitudes (Fossett and Kiecolt 1989; Taylor 1998) and evidence of greater white opposition to government policies that alleviate racial inequality, such as busing (Quillian 1996; Olzak, Shanahan, and West 1994).

These findings supplement research showing a constructive connection between the proportion of African Americans in the general population and whites' with anti-black assertiveness (Fossett and Kiecolt 1989; Taylor 1998) and evidence of countless white disapproval to government procedures that lessen racial disparity, such as busing (Quillian 1996; Olzak, Shanahan, and West 1994). Due to the African American makeup in most areas in the United States, there is not a dramatic change in population from one decade to the next. These outcomes may create longer-lasting effects through the unchanging connotation between race and occupation alignment, which can also determine judicial and political structures when dealing with injustices and inequalities that in the workplace. Research has glaringly suggested that white racism related to the African American population has produced and sustained labor market inequality; however, it is not known how this transmutes into labor market inequality (Cohen and Huffman, 2007). The data that was collected from this study and research designs were considered little help to most according to Reskin (2003) and does not isolate the methods at work, but nonetheless, there is some suggestive evidence. UNC (2007) reported that in 2004, Huffman and Cohen tested whether a positive association between African American and white wage inequality and the percentage of African Americans in local populations were propelled further by job segregation, especially with African American women than by wages that were associated with the black subjugated occupations. In their study, the researchers found that segregation is the likely cause of wage inequality.

Paralleled In contrast to non-managers, managers normally enjoy more notability, job sovereignty, influence, and incomes (Reskin and McBrier 2000; Jacobs 1992). Even though many studies have been

38

conducted on inequality, there is little research focused on management and leadership inequalities with an emphasis on African American women. The research that has been conducted focused on women's entry to administration, frequently with an emphasis on directorial demography (Blau, 1977; Kanter, 1977; Pfeffer 1983). An examination of race and gender inequalities in leadership has not been studied commonly and is a less common concentration of research. A mounting exemplification among secondary groups may intensify mainstream opposition and the inclination to single out individuals (Jacobs 1992; Pfeffer and Davis-Blake 1987).

Effect of Diversity Issues

More women of color have now entered the U.S. workforce according to Gilbert & Ivanecevich (2000); therefore handling diversity successfully has been an emphasis of research inquiries. In 2002, Von Bergen, Soper and Foster defined diversity as the revolution of the population of the United States. In 2005, Lockwood deemed that diversity expands beyond the conventional understanding that once focused mainly on race and gender which shows the bigger viewpoint of workplace diversity currently. Lockwood (2005) stated, "The term diversity has typically referred to women and minorities" (p.7).

Diversity, Inc., an online magazine chooses the top 50 companies for diversity annually. Their research showed that of the top 12 companies selected (the top 10 on the 2005 list plus all companies on the Top 10 Companies for Recruitment & Retention), 3.4% of managers were black women, 1.5% was Latino American and 1.3% was Asian American women (Osuoha, 2010). The article acknowledged that women of color may well continue to come across people who grasp onto stereotypical views of women of color due to their lack of contact and experience with women of color creating diversity issues in the workplace as well as for the organization. In 2003, Howard-Hamilton's study of theoretical frameworks for African American women showed that individuals hold stereotypical views of several occupations centered on psychological and sociological factors (Howard-Hamilton, 2003). Either some people have been programmed to believe through their environment and past experiences, or it is society that formulates their opinions of who should or should not hold various positions within society (Howard-Hamilton, 2003).

A few stereotypes of a more unfavorable nature are that African American women and Latinos do not take criticism well and they are

40

unable to control their emotions (Grin, 2006). As a consequence of these stereotypes, senior management as well as middle management may believe this type of behavior is undesirable, and managers may be less likely to guide or support an African American or a Latino woman to progress in the organization. Therefore management or senior leaders may abstain from delivering beneficial assessment if they think employees of color will not be approachable and welcoming. Johnson (2010) revealed in her study that Tannen (1994), examined the male dominated society and posited that women in positions of authority face a special challenge just because they are women. That challenge directly relates to society's expectations of how a person in authority should behave. The prospect of how individuals in power should act is at odds with outlooks of how a woman, especially a black woman, should behave (Tannen, 1994). Tannen indicated in 1994, "There are different society standards established for the male leader's behavior versus expected behavior of the female leader" (Tannen, 1994). Gyant (1996), in a study of leadership styles of African American civil rights activists, concluded, "A ceiling exists for most African Americans...black skin is still equated by many with a lowering of standards, and nothing much will change that. I don't care how good blacks become…it wouldn't help us" (p18).

Stainback and Tomaskovic-Devey (2006) found minority leadership representation is larger in organizations with more minority employees and they did not control for local population composition, which might drive this connection. Based upon their research of the Equal Employment Opportunity Commission's (EEOC) data from previous years on perceptions of women and people of color which they reviewed, Cohen and Huffman (2007) determined it was challenging to distinguish between the levels of managerial and leadership ability or compensations to managers. An example of this inability to distinguish between the levels of managerial and leadership authority took place in 2006 when Cohen and Huffman could not test whether it was favorable to ensure higher-level management positions, as has been claimed for women.

Gender-Based Barriers

American women consistently face barriers in the workplace especially in corporate America. Many African American women take risks in corporate America, such as Ursula Burns, Chief Executive Officer (CEO) of Xerox. She takes daily risks being in a position that

42

falls under more scrutiny, especially as an African American woman in a position of power. Burns is a rarity. Cook et al. (2002) stated, "The glass ceiling remains omnipresent and many talented employees never reaches their vocational goals because of their race or gender" (p. 303). Redwood (1996) found that sexism, racism, and xenophobia live side-by-side with unemployment, underemployment and poverty; they feed on one another and perpetuate a cycle of unfulfilled aspirations among women and people of color" (Redwood, 1996). Howard-Hamilton (2003) conveyed that individuals have stereotypical interpretations of innumerable professions centered on psychological and sociological factors. These individuals have been encoded to believe that their environment and past experiences or society had formulated their opinions of who should or should not hold various positions within society (Howard-Hamilton, 2003). Johnson (2010) stated, "That challenge directly relates to society's expectations of how a person in authority should behave." Other researchers agree with Johnson's statement regarding the challenges of women, especially African American women. Tannen (1994) believes the expectation of how an individuals in an authoritative role and perceptions along with their own behavior can directly affect another person's morale and ideals, which can come be at odds with expectations of how a woman, especially a black woman, should behave. There are different society standards established for the male leader's behavior versus expected behavior of the female leader (Tannen, 1994). Johnson (2010) conducted a study of African American women in leadership roles in education and concluded that the challenge becomes even greater for the African American female when they have to contend with a male's mindset and perception. Gyant (1996), in a study of leadership styles of African American civil rights activists, concluded, "A ceiling exists for most African Americans...black skin is still equated by many with a lowering of standards, and nothing much will change that. I don't care how good blacks become...it wouldn't help us" (p18). Brunner (1997) posits that all barriers experienced by women in administration are a result either directly or indirectly of an androcentric society. Society has viewed the ideal leader as displaying forceful masculine qualities associated with the behavior of men in formal position of authority (Miller et al., 2006). Patterson (1994), conducted a study on how women shatter glass ceilings in school administration, indicated that White men implicitly describe the dominate culture, thus molding the observations and judgments of society as a man's world. Society views

44

tough, logical, hierarchical control as necessary in leading school districts (Miller et al., 2006). In March 1986, The Wall Street Journal in its Corporate Woman column identified a puzzling new phenomenon (Baxter et al., 2000). According to the article, an obscure but impermeable barrier appeared among a woman and executive positions, thwarting her from reaching the top level in the business world nevertheless of her endeavors and merits (Baxter et al., 2000).

Societal and Cultural Female Functions Characterizations and Expectations

African American women work indefatigably to progress forward in their careers and most prepare themselves socially, educationally, financially, physically and mentally for their careers. However, many African American women are second-guessed about the skills and abilities if they are competent enough to fulfill the essential duties of the position, especially if the position is of a leadership nature (Johnson, 2010). The societal limitations for the African American female are much broader because they include issues of race or racism (Ah Nee-Benham & Cooper, 1998). Societal limitations stem from slavery years ago, therefore setting a tone for stereotypes and class distinctions for African American, especially

African American women. From a historical perspective, the drudgery

work was performed by the un-free, the African American (Mullings,

1997). Mullings (1997) further stated, "One of every three passengers

disembarking from the Atlantic crossing was an African woman, the

one expected to do the drudgery work, one viewed as the second-class

citizen." Preceding World War I, African American women were not

allowed to work in factories which were higher paying occupations,

were originally for white men (until the war). Then white women were

given the opportunity to fulfill the roles of the factory worker while the

men were away at war. The only opportunities that were available for

African Americans especially African American men were

groundskeepers, sharecroppers, farm hands, butlers and janitors.

African American women had even less occupations to choose from,

which they were limited to wet nurses, nannies or maids. African

American women were largely confined to domestic and laundry work

(Mullings, 1997).

It is believed that the cultural training of women has

encouraged them to use consensus management and caring processes to

obtain group goals (Fox-Keller, 1998). In 1986, Gilligan, researched behavioral leadership skills applied by women, which she discovered that women uses relational type leadership skills more often than their male counterparts and that women are great human resource managers and builders (Johnson, 2010). Murtadha and Larson (1999) established in their study of African American women leaders that African American women were viewed as nurturers, compassionate, caring more for individuals than policies. Within the last 15 to 20 years, several questions have been posed concerning women's capabilities to function as a leader, especially in top leadership and managerial roles within organizations due to their nurturing and caring characteristics. Some males consider those characteristics a conflict of interest and could potentially distort one's point of view when a major decision needs to be made in the organization; therefore questions regarding women's ability to be effective leaders are pondered, with this type of scrutiny and questioning, why do so few women, especially African American women reach the top? How can more women leaders reach the top? (Murtadha & Larson, 1999). Regardless of the assortment of studies conducted on women's skills and behaviors that enable women to be effective leaders, they still do not have enough representation as leaders in the workplace, whether it is a small or a large organization, regardless if it is in the private or public sectors. Hemmons (1996) makes it clear that discrimination is an inevitable factor in the life of a black woman, no matter her class, geographic region or family background, but simply because of her race. Hemmons (1996) writes, "Wherever she goes, there are ceilings and whether those ceilings are made of steel, wood or glass, they are there, inflexible, intractable, and impenetrable" (p. 7).

Institutional and Organizational Barriers

Institutional and organizational structures create accesses and barriers for women wanting top administrative roles. Career mobility addresses career opportunities within the institution or organization (Jones & Montenegro, 1982). Johnson (2010) revealed that Jones and Montenegro (1982) identified four predictors significant to career growth and advancement. These predicators are: age; administrative aspirations; clarity of expression; and job experiences. These adaptable prognosticators are classified as having the utmost effect on rising to higher levels within organizations or institutions and occupational success can be most affected by individuals in control of the organization.

Chapter Summary

This literature review provided an historical perspective of all women, including African American women's role in leadership and lack there-of organizations. This chapter also discussed several research studies that focused on the barriers, trials and tribulations that African American women face in the workplace and society. The chapter presented information on how gender, diversity, racial concepts, societal framework and culture has an effect on women, but specifically African American women. Feminist theorists, along with other researchers' views and concepts were also evaluated. Their concepts exhibited leadership traits of African American women. Chapter 3 presents the methodological approaches that will be used for this research study and the population to be studied and will also describe how the data will be gathered along with trustworthiness and cogency of the research instrument to be presented.

CHAPTER THREE: METHODOLOGY

The chapter is organized into three major sections. The first section explains the rationale for selecting the qualitative method to conduct the study and grounded theory. This section includes the key research questions and the justification for using qualitative inquiry, particularly the phenomenological structure to guide the study. Specific matters curtailing from this type of review, such as researcher bias and processes used to authenticate the data, are discussed. The third section explains the data enquiry procedures that will be used to decipher the data obtained from the interviews. The researcher also describes the process that will be used to examine the visceral data for developing themes, and the coding procedure utilized.

Key (1997) defines qualitative research as an investigative method that can be described as ethnographic, naturalistic, anthropological, field, or participant observer research. The second section will explain the methodological approach used, and the justification for using this approach. Qualitative research also stresses the significance of observing variables in the normal setting in which they originate. Therefore, interface amongst variables is imperative, and comprehensive documents are gathered through open-ended questions that give straightforward quotations. According to Jacob (1988), the interviewer is an integral part of the investigation. Smith (1983) states, "This differs from quantitative research which attempts to gather data by objective methods to provide information about relations, comparisons, and predictions and attempts to remove the investigator from the investigation." Qualitative research also uses approaches to evaluate leadership styles and communications, such as observation, interviewing subjects selected for the study, and the use of videoing and recording sessions with the subjects being studied. The advantages of this sampling were the ability to generate data, provide full and revealing sampling, and focus on supportive information vs. forecasted information (Cooper & Schindler, 2003). Qualitative studies assessed for the purpose of this research have been conducted for purposes such as analyzing the leadership and management processes and finding correlations between social background, economical, educational and racial constructs along with leadership styles and the types of influence process used in conjunction with those leadership styles (Conger & Kanungo 1994; Gilbert & Ivancevich, 2000). The grounded theory research method was used for this study in order to investigate the reality-based experiences of the 20 participants selected for the study. Goulding (2003) proposed that grounded theory was intended as an approach for progressing notion that is supported by data, which is methodically composed and analyzed (Goulding, 2003). Grounded theory methodology allowed the researcher to accomplish comprehensive circumstantial investigation of each participant's individual experiences and determine how each one's experiences interrelated, resulting in the development of themes. This methodology further allowed for depictions of the participants' personal experiences and knowledge, therefore aggressively containing them in the study process.

There are some common difficulties related to grounded theory research that includes not knowing when to withdraw from the field and the language of the methodology with it connotations of positivism inherent in terms such as open and axial coding (Goulding, 2003). In 2000, Austen, Jefferson and Therin conducted a pilot study to evaluate the benefits and drawbacks of incorporating significant elements of grounded theory methods in an effort to measure women's social and economic growth. However, their outcomes of the pilot program were not able to dissipate that grounded theory methodology could produce results that were difficult to generalize; they were able to conclude that there are numerous benefits of using a grounded theory method to conduct research on problems pertinent to feminist economics (Johnson, 2006). According to Johnson (2006) in 2003, Austen, Jefferson, and Thein wrote, "An assessment of the data gained through this pilot program also shows that data gathered in a grounded research project can provide a valuable comparison with existing quantitative indicators" (p. 15). Johnson (2006) also researched Kushner and Morrow's perception of the grounded theory methodology, which Kushner and Morrow (2003) stated, "Grounded theory method may allow-but does not compel-researchers to extend their consideration of structural influences on social processes to depth analysis of the setting and context of intermediate and macro social organization"(p. 37). The writers determined that critical theory and feminism theory as critical approaches have extended progresses in grounded theory as well as interpretative practices to aid the mixing of socio structural examination in regards to rationalizations of human contact in the social world.

Methodological Approach

A qualitative approach using a grounded theory research method was used to conduct this study that enabled the researcher the chance to use real-life situations and experiences of the study participants. A qualitative approach allowed qualitative data to provide depth and detail through direct quotation and description of situations, events and interactions, and allows the researcher to assess leadership styles and communications employed measures such as interviewing, case studies, observations and micro aspects. Consequential to receiving organizational approval, potential study participants' demographic, educational and employment information were reviewed, based on North Carolina state governmental Business Intelligence (BI) reports were run to confirm eligibility criteria for the study were met. This criteria-based analysis provided demographic information that pertains to the study and the participants, such as education, their current and past work levels, pay, their managers and their direct and indirect reports and, if applicable, their mentors.

Selection of Participants

The study focused on 18 African American women in leadership as managers and/or leaders in a predominantly White, male-dominant culture in state government. The study identified factors that could potentially contribute to the low representation, within the respective organization of the 18 African American women managers/leaders, within such a culture. One of the objectives of this research study was to focus on 18 African American women in leadership roles to determine if there is identicalness. Another objective of this study was to further the current body of knowledge pertaining to inequalities of the workplace and the interactions of gender, race and pay for African American women.

Grounded theory research method was used to examine significant encounters identifiable to each of the study participants in their own individual, personal and professional workplace occurrences. Appropriate approval from each participant's organization were obtained in writing via e-mail from the participants' respective organizations and the approval came from the participants' immediate supervisors to participate in the study. Furthermore, the supervisors did not know which of their employees had been selected and allowed the principal researcher to select the participants on their own. This was verbally agreed upon between the principal researcher and the supervisors.

Five research questions were formed for this study in order to encapsulate the personal experiences of the study participant's professional and personal experiences in their own words. The questions were developed to address the research basis, the information needed to achieve the study purpose, and the viability that the research questions would be addressed. The research questions were also designed to capture the study participants' own personal and professional experiences pertaining to influential factors such as social and economic exposure and background, sources of inspiration, demographic and or situational strategies, leadership characteristics and obstacles on personal and professional level.

The principal research notified study participants via phone calls at their work locations that they have been selected to be participants in a study focused on African American women leaders and managers in organizational leadership in North Carolina state government; their work phone numbers were obtained from the NC governmental BI reporting database. The study participants were informed via phone calls by the principal researcher with a brief overview of what the study entailed and answered any immediate questions and addressed any concerns that the study candidate may have had at that time. The researcher also verbally notified the participants that they may withdraw from the study at any time during the study. Also additional contact information such as the principal researcher's personal E-mail address and cell phone number was given to the study participants. The study participant was given the opportunity to exchange personal E-mail and home addresses, and/or cell phone numbers to be contacted when needed. The researcher also e-mailed a consent form to the participant's home address along with a stamped envelope with the researcher's home address to return the consent form to the researcher. This was done so the participant could give their consent to participate in the research study, not only verbally, but to have the consent in written documentation.

Interviews were conducted using a Sony ICD BX112 2GB digital voice recorder to document the responses to the interview questions, along with notes taken by the researcher while the interview was being conducted. There was no time limit for the interviews; this method allowed the participants to take their time in relaying responses to the researcher and strengthen the validity of the study. The interviews were conducted on the Northern Wake County Campus of Wake Technical Community College, Office 203, in Raleigh, North Carolina. The office setting was a quiet environment with two chairs, a desk, a window, and the office had adequate lighting. There was no constant traffic in the office itself and its immediate location, and was a neutral location for the researcher and the participants and was not occupied by any faculty or staff members of the college. Each interview question was formed to focus on the research and the erudition needed to accomplish the purpose of the study and the feasibility that research questions would be addressed in order to identify the barriers and challenges perceived to be encountered in the workplace by African American women seeking leadership/managerial roles. The statistical data researched was based on the following criteria:

1. Participant must have had two years or more of management experience, either in private or public sector and has applied and or interviewed for a higher position in management within the past 5 years.

2. Participant must be employed with the North Carolina state government for two years for the governmental portion of the research.

3. Participants for the private sector must be employed with their organization for two years for the private sector portion of the research, regardless if they have been in their managerial roles for the two years or not.

4. Education of any level which includes high school or college (individuals that attended college will not have to have a degree).

5. All sociocultural backgrounds (societal norms may vary for each participant).

6. All economic backgrounds accepted (poor, middle and upper class economic background of each participant).

7. Additional training or certifications received within the past 5 years.

8. Must be an African American woman between the ages of 25 and 65.

Study Population

The study focused on and described the trials and tribulations of 18 African American women in leadership roles in the public sector and explored the employment experiences of these diverse group of proficient and qualified women in the workplace as they bid to escalate into their prospective management and leadership roles in governmental entities. The sample size was 18 African American women in management/leadership roles in the public sector of North Carolina state government between the ages of 25 and 65 years old and the sampling strategy and approach used was quota sampling. From the criteria above and the BI reporting, the participants will be chosen from three separate North Carolina governmental state agencies. The first state agency employs 200 hundred people, and three participants are from this agency. The second state agency employs 4,000 people, and 10 participants are from this agency and the third state agency employs 19,210 individuals, and five individuals are participants. The purpose of conducting statistical and query research via reports is to establish eligibility criteria for the study and confirmation that the criterion has been met for the study. The benchmark-based analysis will provide demographic material affecting the participants of the study and their managers and if pertinent their manager's supervisor.

Purpose of Analysis

This analysis focused on individual personal motivations, morals, success factors, barriers such as race, diversity issues, gender differences and leadership capabilities and practices and the impact that these items has on the women. Four research questions were established for this study in order to gain insight on the professional and personal experiences and occurrences of the participants in their own words and descriptions. Each question was formed to focus on the research and the erudition needed to accomplish the purpose of the study and according to Robson (2002), "the feasibility that research questions would be addressed." The research questions allowed the identification of barriers and challenges perceived to be encountered in the workplace by African American women seeking leadership/managerial roles. The research questions also allowed the participants of the study to voice their opinions and share in their own words their immediate experiences on sources of inspiration, influential factors, strategies and leadership characteristics. The goal of this study was to provide answers and possible solution to the all-encompassing question: What are the perceptions of African American women about their barriers and trials in rising to leadership and managerial roles in the workplace?

Qualitative Inquiry

Merriam (1998) defines qualitative research as an "umbrella concept covering several forms of inquiry that help us understand and explain the meaning of social phenomena with as little disruption of the natural setting as possible" (p. 5). Myers (2000) defines qualitative methods as instruments used in understanding and describing the world of human experiences. Myers also states that a key force of the qualitative approach is the depth to which investigations are conducted along with descriptions of the study and explanations are written, usually resulting in adequate details for the reader to comprehend the full breadth of the situation. The definitive intention of qualitative research is to propose a perspective of a situation and give well-written research reports that display the researcher's ability to illustrate or describe the corresponding phenomenon (Myers, 2000). The main goals of this study were to:

1. Explore through the interview process the perceptions of African American women in the workplace and the barriers and challenges in ascending to leadership roles within their organizations.

2. To learn more about the African American women who serve in leadership roles and how their experiences have shaped who they are as leaders.

When assessing this research study from a wide view, Myers' explanation of qualitative studies best satisfies the principal goals of this study. Merriam (1998) describes qualitative research as an "umbrella concept covering several forms of inquiry that help us understand and explain the meaning of social phenomena with as little disruption of the natural setting as possible" (p. 5). This research encompasses the five properties defined by Merriam as developing the foundation of qualitative research. These are:

1. Reality is formed by individuals interacting with their social world.

2. The research is the foremost instrument for data collection and analysis.

3. Fieldwork is usually conducted.

4. An inductive research strategy is mainly employed.

5. The product of a qualitative study is richly descriptive (p. 8).

Protection of Human Subjects

Interview responses were anonymous, and all information submitted will be and shall remain confidential. Interview responses from participants have been stored on a Kingston Data Traveler flash drive and the Sony ICD BX112 2GB Digital voice recorder device that contains a micro tape, which will remain in the researcher's possession and stored in a safe deposit box with SunTrust Bank in Raleigh, North Carolina. All data will be discarded six years after the completion of the study. The study will not cause any harm nor put the participants at risk of losing their employment at their designated work locations and organizations. Participants will not seek any financial compensation for their involvement in the study and also will have the option to freely withdraw from the study at any given time.

Instrumentation

The data collection instrument that was developed for this study was an interview guide (see Appendix C). The guide contains open-ended questions on a semi-structured basis that focused on the participants' personal experiences in the workplace while climbing the ladder in management and leadership. The interview questions, eliminating the questions pertaining to demographic information are similar to the research study by Dr. Jennie Porter (2002), titled, "An Investigation of the Glass Ceiling in Corporate America: The Perspective of African American women." The demographic information will be collected through the BI queries generated to evaluate the participants that would be eligible for the study.

The interview guide is the data collection method applied to capture the detailed responses relating to professional and personal experiences of the study participants. The interview guide enabled the researcher to assemble data in person, orally by utilizing a small representative population. The same interview guide was used for each participant while conducting the interview and documented responses as given assisted the researcher in managing unfairness and influence. The use of this instrumentation also allowed the researcher to know if additional in-depth responses were needed or to direct the discussion to guarantee that all subjects on the interview guide were covered.

Trustworthiness

Maxwell (2005) discourses the significance of creditability when conducting an academic study. He reveals that the term validity is most often correlated with the quantitative paradigm, and is not the best term to associate with qualitative study. Maxwell also mentions that the word validity is most often related to the quantitative paradigm, and is not the best term to associate with qualitative study. Johnson (2010) stated, "When conducting a study that uses a qualitative method, it is imperative to make sure that the data assembled and conclusions generated from the data have a strong awareness of creditability and trustworthiness." Johnson (2010) further states, "Data generated in the qualitative paradigm involves the lived experiences of individuals." Maxwell (2005) prefers to use the term verification, as it infers that the techniques used in qualitative studies can have the needed meticulousness, while still upholding the individual's official encounters. The methods used for verification was the use of cross-referencing and participant de-briefing. In order to be un-biased from affecting the study, the recordings from the interview were examined by listening to them. The researcher listened to the recordings three times with two finished transcriptions for exactness and familiarity

66

proceeding to coding and analyzing the data. Cross-referencing the themes that emerged from the data with the themes that were examined in the literature was compared with the themes between the transcripts of the different participants interviewed in the study and similarities or differences that may be related to age or geographical location of the participants as a cross reference between the participants was also evaluated.

Chapter Summary

The researcher's interest in the under representation of African American women in leadership and managerial roles in organizations whether it is the private or public sector, probed an investigation of possible factors that is causing the glass ceiling effect. A qualitative method approach was used to discover this issue. In chapter III, a definition of the under representation of African American women in management and leadership has been established along with the type of research method that was used, theoretical framework, participant selection, instrumentation, ethical considerations, data analysis and trustworthiness. Chapter IV presents the outcomes of the study and Chapter V presents analysis, inferences, confines, and suggestions for additional research represented from the results.

CHAPTER FOUR: RESULTS

Introduction

Regardless of the research endeavors of womanist theologians, leadership philosophers and feminists along with a progressively more varied workforce than in the preceding years, an under-representation of African American women in leadership and managerial roles and positions in the workplace still remains compared to a White male-dominated representation in the workplace and remains an issue. The purpose of this study was to describe the trials and tribulations of 18 African American women in leadership roles in the public sector and explore the employment experiences of this diverse group of proficient and qualified women in the workplace as they bid to escalate into their prospective management and leadership roles not only in corporate America, but in governmental entities as well. This analysis focused on individual personal motivations, morals, success factors, barriers such as race, diversity issues, gender differences and leadership capabilities and practices and the impact that these items has on the women.

This study examined the exclusive individual and professional views, expressions and opinions and experiences of African American women in leadership and or managerial roles in North Carolina state government working in a White-male dominated culture. Particularly, the study pursued to ascertain whether African American women working in such a culture had similarities and agreed in their acuities of inequalities and factors that contribute to African American women low representation in leadership and managerial roles and positions in North Carolina State government. The goal of this study was to apprehend how the existing realisms relate to workplace disparities and the connections of gender, race, social-economic background and education for the 18 African American women and present an inclusive analysis of recognized apprehensions and possibly to lead organizations to rethink their current processes in regards to hiring practices, training, assessment of employees or future employees; become more culturally diverse in the work place; and develop some possible resolutions in order to weaken those trepidations and increase reassurances of removal of barriers and a diverse workforce.

Description of Participants' Backgrounds

A total of 18 participants working in a White, male-dominated culture in three different North Carolina state governmental agencies were interviewed for this research study. Explicitly, the participants work within human resources, education and rehabilitation/social services fields, and all participants are at the managerial level or higher. Specifically, three directors (30%) and 15 managers (70%), were interviewed for this study.

Table 1 provides a descriptive outline of the participants' backgrounds. To assist in comprehending the table, the researcher presents the resulting explanations. OBTAINED encapsulates how the study participant acquired their present positions. MGLDEXP captures the particular amount of managerial and/or leadership experience the study participants had before the study. The number of individuals who reported to the participants as subordinates are categorized as ranges in DIRECTS. Mentor means the study participant currently has a mentor, and Mentee shows the study participant currently has a mentee that she is mentoring in her organization. FORMMTEE means the study participant was a former mentee in a mentoring program.

Table 1 demonstrated an amount of substantial arrangements of information. For example, all the participants reported to a White supervisor; eight (10%) reported to a female supervisor and 10 (90%) participants reported to a male supervisor, thus corroborating the White, male-dominated culture within their respective organizations. Also, none of the participants (100%) has a mentor; two participants

(20%) currently have mentees; 16 participants (80%) do not have mentees; 16 (80%) of the participants have not been in a mentoring program; and two participants (20%) have participated in a mentoring program in their respective organizations. Three study participants hold high school diplomas; two participants hold Associate degrees; five participants hold Bachelor's degrees; five hold Master's degrees; one participant holds a Master of Business Administration (MBA); one participant holds a Doctor of Philosophy (PhD); and one participant holds a Doctor of Education (EdD). The women's managerial and or leadership experience ranges from three to 25 years.

Table 1

Part cip	Part cip Age	Supervi sor's Gender	Supervi sor's Race	Obtain ed	MGLD EXP	Dir ects	Edu Lvl	Me ntor	Men tee	FOR MM TEE
P1	38	F	W	Job Posting	3	5	High Sch Dip	No	No	No
P2	56	F	W	Job Posting	8	2	Bachel or's	No	Yes	No
P3	55	F	W	Netwo rking	8	6	Bachel or's	No	Yes	Yes
P4	41	M	W	Netwo rking	12	2	High Sch Dip	No	No	No
P5	49	F	W	Other	13	6	Maste r's	No	No	No
P6	48	F	W	Job Posting	5	7	Maste r's	No	No	No
P7	47	M	W	Other	7	4	Maste r's	No	No	No
P8	45	F	W	Job Posting	24	7	High Sch Dip	No	No	No
P9	36	M	W	Job Posting	15 yrs	1	EdD	No	No	No
P10	42	M	W	Other	18 yrs	15	Maste r's	No	No	No
P11	43	M	W	Other	5 yrs	10	Bachel or's	No	No	No
P12	63	F	W	Netwo rking	25 yrs	8	PhD	No	No	Yes
P13	28	M	W	Job Posting	2 yrs	2	Maste r's	No	No	No
P14	37	M	W	Job Posting	8 yrs	8	Associ ate's	No	No	No
P15	36	M	W	Other	3 yrs	3	Associ ate's	No	No	No
P16	35	M	W	Netwo rking	2 yrs	4	MBA	No	No	No
P17	59	F	W	Job Posting	23 yrs	1	Bachel or's	No	No	No
P18	34	M	W	Job Posting	12	3	Bachel or's	No	No	No

Demographic Analysis

Business Intelligence (BI) reports were compiled from the Systems Applications and Products (SAP) / Human Resource Information Management (HRIM) system that North Carolina State governmental agencies use for human resources, benefits, time management and payroll reporting with the permission of the state Controller to determine the selection of the research study participants. After the results from the BI reports were assembled and analyzed, the selected candidates for the study were invited verbally in person, by phone or e-mail to participate in the study. The information obtained from the BI reports also assisted in collecting the demographic data used in this study and was entered in a statistical program, SPSS, which is a data editor to analyze the quantitative area of data of the study in order to classify the information (IBM, 2013). The procedure of SPSS allowed the data analysis to be performed using cross tabulations and creating frequency tables. By carrying out the cross tabulations technique, pictorial charts representing different combinations of the demographic significances for two or more variables to be tabulated were formed. The creation of frequency tables demonstrated how often the participants gave each reply. The specific demographic variables pertained to the following items: ethnicity; gender; education levels; participants' ages; method of which the participants learned of their position; time of transition periods from a subordinate role to supervisory status (either as a manager or in a leadership capacity); number of subordinates reporting directly to the participants, history of participants as mentors and mentees.

This demographic data then was analyzed in order to identify possible influential factors whether it be situational or demographic, within the dominant culture in their respective organization that may have evolved based on the participants' educational, social and workplace experiences. Another was to identify possible influential factors (situational or demographic) that may have guided or impeded career advancement of the participants, and to identify sources of motivation that may have influenced the participants' leadership development.

Data Collected

The sample size is 18 African American women in management and or leadership roles in the public sector of NC state government between the ages of 25-65 years old, and the sampling strategy and approach used is quota sampling. Quota sampling allowed a demand on who is to be sampled known as targeting (Changing

Minds, 2012). This process was used because of the potential difficulty

in recruiting African American women in managerial and or leadership

roles in a White, male-dominated culture. After the gathering of

demographic data had been analyzed, the selected candidates for the

study were contacted by phone, e-mail or in person regarding the study;

given details on how they were chosen and what the study consisted of.

During this interaction between the researcher and selected candidates,

participants were given the opportunity to participate in the study,

where the candidate had an opportunity to reply yes or no, or took time

to think about participating. The researcher then mailed informed

consent forms (see Appendix D) to the selected individuals' homes

with the details of the study and a signature line to sign and date giving

their consent to participate and a return self-stamped envelope so the

participants can return the consent form to the researcher. After the

forms were returned to the researcher, follow up emails or phone calls

were made to set up an interview time at the designated neutral

location. Fifteen of the 18 interviews were conducted face to face; one

interview was done via Face Time; and two interviews were conducted

via e-mail due to some participants and the researcher's conflicting work schedules. Each interview was audio recorded using a Sony ICD BX112 2GB digital recorder to document the responses to the 25 interview questions, and each interview time varied between 45 minutes to one hour and 15 minutes.

Data Analysis

Interviews were recorded using a digital recorder and transcribed precisely by the researcher. The researcher also allowed the participants to review a copy of their transcribed interviews in order to verify the correct replication of their interview responses. After each participant reviewed and approved the transcribed data from the interview, the data was processed using QDA Miner Lite, a qualitative data analysis software program, to assist with qualitative data analysis and categorizing. QDA Miner Lite provided instruments that allowed the data to be arranged as paradigms into mutual categories, express theoretical and empirical relations, and visualize convoluted relations among perceptions.

The responses of the participants were used to develop subject matter descriptions to formulate correlations between classes and to assist in exposing relations among categories (Beyer & Hannah, 2002; Kushner & Morrow, 2003; Austen, Jefferson, & Thein, 2003). QDA

Miner Lite was further used to assist with the formulation of themes and theme codes based on information of themes and them codes based on information obtained through the interviews. Participant responses to interview guide questions and the related issues that arose during the interview process were reviewed and segmented as complete quotations and categorized according to the topic or issue addressed in the research question. The QDA Miner Lite software helped align theme codes to one or more themes, dependent upon the participants' spoken intent.

The content analysis of the interview data was completed manually and with computer assistance in order to verify alignment of the finding, and responses were analyzed thematically using QDA Miner Lite, which enabled the data to be readily grouped by related themes from different transcripts. This software helped determine whether there were similarities or differences of views on specific issues and to identify the number of times issues were raised and any thematic linkages. Derived from paraphrasing of common experiences, direct quotes and the themes that were emerged were ranked by their frequency of mention and categorized by topic. These themes formed a comprehensive representation of the participant's experience being

78

investigated. The participants' experiences were communicated through their own interpretation. Therefore, the exact experience and its meaning to the individual who had it were analyzed. In previous research, this process was defined as lived experiences, and the stories and narratives that people share about them and their world (Ingram & Moule, 2001). In 2002, Mehra suggested that researcher bias enters into the picture even if the researcher tries to stay out of it. To address the issue of researcher bias, the researcher used the bracketing approach. The bracketing approach allowed the researcher to set aside the question of the real existence of the contemplated object as well as all other questions about its physical or objective nature (Phenomenology Research, 2011). The researcher, understanding how her own personal gender and ethnicity could bias the interview, kept a constant mental reiteration that the participants' view and experiences belonged to them and prevented her from performing the interviews with any predetermined judgments. This approach allowed for the identification of the researcher's preconceived ideas and assumptions about the phenomenon under investigation and allowed the researcher to set them aside while still providing instigation for a more emotional response from the participant (Iwasaki, MacKay, & Mactavish, 2005).

Themes and Theme Codes

The participant's names and organization names that were mentioned and used for this study were changed in order to maintain anonymity. Through qualitative data analysis, similarities or differences of views on specific topics, the number of times issues were raised, and any thematic linkages were examined. Each data file was treated as a separate source, and the data were then segmented into marked-up portions of the source document. Due to the QDA Minor Lite data analysis, 11 themes emerged from the source data and from direct quotes and paraphrasing of common experiences. Table 2 provides an illustrative look at these themes.

Table 2

Career Pathway	Cultural Deficits
Diversity/Fairness	Gender/Race Interaction
Leadership	Mentoring
Own Leadership Style	Personal Challenges
Professional Challenges	Strategies/Advice
Success	

A code editor created the codes that evolved and the codes were based on people, places and events. Codes that were based on people were attributed to gender and race and codes were also attributed to time. Various themes had numerous codes because they spanned categories and because the themes were not conjointly exclusive, redundancy was inevitable. In order to circumvent this type of recurrence in the written analysis, specific extracts were used only once. Table 3 supports an illustrative look at the themes that developed and the number of theme codes that were connected with the identifiable theme.

Table 3

Development of Themes and Theme Codes

THEMES ASSOCIATED	NUMBER OF THEME CODES	THEMES ASSOCIATED	NUMBER OF THEME CODES
Career Pathway	39	Cultural Deficits	11
Diversity/Fairness	15	Gender/Race Interaction	4
Leadership	9	Mentoring	1
Own Leadership Style	10	Personal Challenges	3
Professional Challenges	9	Strategies/Advice	42
Success	4		

After a thorough review of the themes and their respective

theme codes, the researcher aligned the themes with the four research

questions. The alignment of the questions with the themes was based

on the themes typically associated to the question being addressed. For

example, research question number 4 had the greatest number of themes, and 36% associated to the issues being addressed in its

question. Research questions 1 and 3 had the least number of themes,

2% associated to the issues being addressed in the questions. The

remaining research question number 2 had an equal number of themes

with 18% associated to the issues being addressed in the questions.

Table 4 displays the alignments.

Table 4

Research Question and Theme Code Alignments

Question #	Research Question	Theme
1	What are the leadership characteristics of African American women serving in leadership roles, such as in upper management in organizations?	Leadership Own Leadership Style
2	Is there a significant difference in the leadership behavior and style of African American women leaders versus White, Hispanic and Asian women and White, Hispanic and Asian males and what are the differences if any?	Gender/Race Interaction Mentoring Approaches/Advice
3	Do you believe there is a relationship between educational levels of African American women employees who elevates to the highest positions in the workplace in the United States and the African American women who do not receive advancements and what type of relationship levels are there?	Career Pathway Success
4	Does economic and social background, such as coming from a poor, middle or upper class setting play a deciding factor in an African American woman's ability to obtain a leadership role in an organization and could you explain in detail the reason for your response?	Cultural Deficits Diversity/Fairness Personal Challenges Professional Challenges

The chart information is further discussed as individual research questions findings and broken down into specific themes associated with the research question. Some of the theme codes that appeared more often than others were identified.

Research Question 1 Findings

Research question number 5 implored data from the participants pertaining to their leadership physiognomies that have developed within their organization and their organization's culture. As outlined in Table 4, the leadership style themes mostly lined up with this research question, and two theme codes emerged from this question. These two theme codes pertained to elements, leadership style and principles.

Leadership Theme

Participants associated several elements and or styles to becoming a successful leader. They believed that a successful manager and leader should motivate, be trustworthy, be fair and consistent, and be a visionary, responsible and be an effective communicator. All the participants felt that without those attributes, you cannot be successful as a manager and or leader and without these attributes you may have a high turnover rate in the workplace. Building and fostering good relationships internally and externally is also very important to being an effective leader.

Participants' Own Leadership Style Theme

Each participant identified their individual leadership style and how their style came about. Several leadership styles emerged from the research question, and 98 percent of the participants have at least one leadership style in common, democratic leadership. This leadership theme style is noted as being the most effective leadership style due to this style offering guidance and participation from the leader in a group setting. The participants noted that their leadership styles evolved from numerous factors such as their cultural and ethical background, education, training and experience. Some participants expressed how they exhibit their leadership style(s) in the workplace by leading by example. One participant made sure she always participated in work-related on-site activities such as dressing up for Halloween and a Christmas cubicle/office decorating contest to show her staff that she is a team player. Several participants felt that reliability was a significant link to believability and they are careful to uphold reliability and integrity as well as have some type of value-based principles.

Research Question 2 Findings

Research question number 2 implored data from the participants pertaining to their own approaches and advice they have developed inside and outside the workplace regarding gender/race interaction and mentoring.

Gender/Race Interaction Theme

Although only a few theme codes evolved from the participants' responses related to this theme, the two primary ones were race and gender. There was a tremendous agreement that race and gender continue to play a significant role in career advancement. One participant declared, "I feel that women in general have a difficult time breaking the barrier in the workplace, and when you're African American women, it's even harder for you to break those silos and climb the corporate ladder and overcome those barriers." Another participant stated, "I still see and feel racial overtones in my immediate workplace. I feel we're (African American women and Latinas) always stereotyped, so that's why I try my best not to live up to their expectations of what they perceived me to be." Another added, "Racism and sexism are still real, apparent and visible, and from time to time, rears its ugly head at work."

The participants were aligned in their perceptions in that there is still opportunity for improvement. Although efforts to diminish subtle and overt prejudices have aided in some progress to change organizational culture, decisions are still being made based on instantaneous assumptions, examinations and opinions. One participant stated, "Some people still make decisions based upon their own immediate observations, and they make assumptions based on those personal observations." Another participant stated, "No one is foolish and reckless as they once were in the workplace, because with the various laws and policies and procedures that's out here, people can file a report whether it's civil or criminal and be brought up on charges internally or externally. These days you'll be placed under investigation at work with or without pay for people doing silly stuff at work."

Another participant said, "Surely, my White contemporaries had no respect for trying to get minorities and women more conventional, they really didn't and had no shame in doing so." Another participant stated, "Every so often I think we (African Americans) are perceived as being a little tougher and take no mess." One other participant stated,

"I have observed that in meetings or general conversation with some of the members of senior management, especially the White males in senior management, hesitates or become more reserved when I make a suggestion and or come up with an idea. They hesitate because they're judging my ability to carry out this task and also silently questioning my strength and knowledge. They already have a visual perception of my ability to perform my job and duties. Had I been a White or an Asian woman, I would not get the hesitation that I have and still receive. This is also how I know: I've been stereotyped, and racism is still prevalent in the work environment."

Some of the participants believe that African American women must live a dual life at work. One participant stated, "I feel that I must conform at work as well as outside of work when interacting to co-workers. If I don't conform, they may judge me and see me in a different light." One participant stated that at times she feels alone in her workplace, especially since she is the only African American woman in her area in addition, there aren't a lot of women period in the workplace. She also stated that she often finds herself walking on eggshells because she is not sure what to say or how to dress, based on past instances where she was told because of her ethnic background, her dress may be perceived a "little too provocative," and she sometimes "comes off too snappy." Once she was given that information, she became more quiet and subdued. Another participant stated that she repressed her culture by wearing her hair ways that White corporate America would find acceptable in order to fit in and feel accepted in the workplace. When she first started in state government years ago, she had natural hair and loved it. She had locks and kept them up very well, but she would notice that she would get sideways glances and stares from her white counterparts. Some African American and sometimes the White co-workers would have questions and always wanted to touch her hair. Therefore, she found this quite annoying and decided to cut her hair. She did regret the cutting but she stills remain natural and wears her hair in natural hair styles such as an Afro from time to time, which she still receives some stares but not like when she had her locks.

One participant overheard a White female manager tell another manager that she has had some challenges with her African American female employees. The participant further stated the White female manager said, "They're awfully direct at times and can come across as being condescending, and at times I don't know if they're joking or being serious, so I don't know what to say or do sometimes." Participants also described other situations where they felt their intellect was questioned; it's a perception that African Americans have less intellect than other races. One participant remembers teaching a class to individuals in various North Carolina state governmental agencies and a White woman stated to her, "I didn't know that you are smart as you are! Wow, I would have not thought that you were this smart and the education that you have!" The participant said she did not know how to respond to the student's comments, and she was even more stunned that the comments came out of the woman's mouth. The participant stated that all she could do was force a smile and say thank you and walk away. The participant said she walked away because she was fuming. She really wanted to ask the student what was meant by her comments and set the woman straight. She decided to take the higher road because sometimes people say certain things just to get under your skin. As soon as she would have went off, "sista-girl" mode would have been in full effect and she did not want to give the student anything negative to say about her and feed into the "African American women has attitude" hype.

All of the participants said that they had a certain degree of difficulty addressing work-related prejudices and stereotypes within their respective organizations. Two participants stated that they felt nervous, as well as doubtful, that anything would come of bringing up a topic such as prejudice. They also did not want to be seen as trouble makers. One participant raised the idea of prejudice in a staff meeting and was told if she had any issues with being discriminated against, she should talk with the ER (Employee Representative) and voice her concerns and opinions there. Another participant also brought the same topic up directly in a one-on-one conversation with her supervisor, who is a White male; he told her that maybe she should seek EAP (Employee Assistance Program) for counseling sessions about the issue and the way she felt, regarding prejudices and stereotypes. The participant stated, "I was floored by his response. I asked him was he serious and he looked at me and said, 'Yes.' I knew then, I was not going to get any assistance in this matter, so I either could keep quiet and go on or I could really cause a ruckus and possibly lose my job, so I decided to keep quiet for now. However, I'm documenting everything that goes on."

Mentoring Theme

All participants identified that having a mentor is important and that individual recognizes their skills, abilities and knowledge as well as talent in performing their job and duties. Superiors are the ones to notice an individual's potential and drive, therefore moving one up the ranks and also securing this individual's role in the organization. However, all 18 participants have never been a mentor in the workplace, two are currently in a mentoring program in the workplace and two were former mentees (see table 2). Even though the majority of the participants have never been mentors, a mentee or currently in a mentoring program, the participants stated that their direct supervisors or another supervisor has provided them with some words of wisdom and advice on success and being successful in the workplace, whether the information given was warranted or not. Four participants sought their own mentors, and the 14 other participants chose not to because they did not see anyone in their work environment that they considered mentoring worthy. All 18 participants showed a deep interest in mentoring other African American women, especially the young ones that are just starting out in the workforce and state government to assist them in transition. They showed interest in wanting to encourage the young women, especially those who are transitioning from the private sector, and let them know they have someone in their corner if they have questions and or need advice. One participant stated that when her boss found out that she was "unofficially" mentoring a 20-year old

African American woman who just started with her team, she was called into the office and questioned on her motives. The participant told the supervisor her reasons for doing so and the supervisor told her next time to ask if she could do something like that. Furthermore, her supervisor asked to be informed of the mentee's progress. Subsequently, her boss told their superior and the participant's boss received all the credit for having her mentor the young woman. The participant said, "I was so hurt and upset, but I shouldn't be surprised that happened, especially here at my agency." The participant further stated, "I don't regret mentoring that young lady, who was also in college full time and working with me full time. That young lady graduated college, received her Master's degree and is now a supervisor in the same agency, just in a different location in the state. Every time I see this young lady 'til this day, she thanks me for helping her and giving her guidance and the strength to carry on." I may have gotten my hand popped for what I did initially, but I certainly do not regret it."

In reviewing the responses of the participants on this topic, it was apparent that they believe that having a mentor is needed and proves to be valuable and could help careers in the long run, whether it

94

is an established mentoring program or unofficially taking someone under your wing. Specific growth areas for mentoring were also identified that pertained to the type of work being conducted by the mentee. Everyone should have a mentor of some sort for at least the first 90 days of employment at the minimum and some participants said new employees, especially if they are new to state government, should be mentored for at least a year.

Approaches /Advice Theme

All participants supported giving advice to other African American women that desire to go into management and leadership. The participants' advice consisted of reliability, expansion of knowledge and abilities, work ethic, office politics, and guiding and counseling others in the workplace.

The participants believed that being reliable is very important, especially being an African American woman, specifically since African Americans are stereotyped frequently as being delayed in arriving for appointments, work, etc. One participant noted that punctuality is key to making it up the ranks and corporate ladder. Another participant noted that, "If you're on time, you're late." All participants agreed that office politics should be avoided at all costs but advocated for staying true to individual values and principles. The participants also agreed that those who wish to become managers and or leaders should broaden their horizons, be hard workers, make suggestions in the workplace, be team players, contributors, and expand their knowledge base in their respective fields and even furthering their education (not necessarily obtaining a degree, but obtaining certifications in different areas).

All participants suggested that individuals interested in management and leadership should become involved in professional organizations or non-profit organizations to aid with networking and to help with mentoring opportunities if they are not receiving any type of guidance and counsel ship in the workplace. Outside organizations may consist of church groups, sororities, school organizations such as honor societies and women peer groups. Other suggestions from the participants included not burning bridges, removing oneself from the immediate work space and walking to another area or department when stressed or upset, and always stay informed on what is going on in the workplace. One participant noted that you need to make yourself visible in the workplace from time to time. Go to another department so other co-workers can know who you are and make alliances with these individuals. The same participant also stated, "When I first started my job, I didn't move from my cubicle, I was a bit stand-offish, because I am somewhat shy, but I made myself walk around after being in the workplace for three weeks and meet people in different areas. I'm glad I used this approach because; I was able to learn more about the organization as well as learn about different job and training opportunities in and outside of the workplace. It's all about networking and letting people know who you are and what you do and can do."

Education also was a highly favored topic amongst the participants. Fifteen participants have at least one degree (97 percent), and three participants (3 percent) only have a high school diploma (see Table 1). The three participants that have only have a high school diploma also have various certifications such as a Notary license and management certifications. Two participants stated that they will pursue furthering their education within the next six months. All participants said that education is key, it's important and everyone should seek education, whether it's in the classroom or you're reading a book or participating in webinars to gain more knowledge in your field or another area and advise that all African American women utilize education as an important tool in advancing their careers.

When reviewing the responses to this research question, it was apparent that all the participants provided and offered advice and approaches based upon their own personal experiences and encounters. It was also clear-cut that their mutual views value making a difference in African American women's lives and suggesting that educating yourself is one of the keys to success and all of the participants admitted that without an education, especially those with advance degrees would not be as successful as they are in the workplace.

Research Question 3 Findings

Research question number 3 was aligned with participants' information pertaining to the relationship between educational levels of African American women employees and the influential factors that may obstruct their career progression.

Career Pathway Theme

Career path and success were the themes that emerged from the participants' responses to the research question. Thirteen participants chose their career paths, and five participants did not choose their current career path. The 13 participants that chose their career paths knew that they wanted to be employed in an organization where they could utilize their skills that they have obtained whether it was skills obtained through higher education and/or on-the-job training. The five participants that did not choose their current career paths were deployed from other positions within NC state government in order to have a job due to their current positions being abolished due to budget cuts or other organizational reasons. Ninety-five percent of the participants acquired their positions by applying and interviewing for their current positions and becoming the selected candidate. Five percent of the participants knew someone in their organization that were in a hiring role and were offered a position, and they accepted the position.

All participants agreed that their vast backgrounds impacted their career paths, whether it was educationally motivated or based primarily on their knowledge, skills and abilities. Seventy percent stated their upbringing had something to do with their career path, and 30 percent said that their personal and professional experiences prepared them for their current managerial and leadership roles along with lessons learned from personal and professional obstacles.

Success Theme

The success theme code is about the meaning of success to the participants and what contributing factors leads to being successful. All of the participants had their own views and opinions on success, but one commonality among all the participants was that they believed that an individual must be authentic. Another common theme of success noted amongst all the participants is a level of readiness. The participants believed that an individual must be prepared and ready at all times, in and outside of the workplace, in order to become and remain successful, especially for an African American woman. Some participants confessed that their views on success have changed from what they originally thought. One participant stated when she was in her early 20s, she thought money and being a high-powered executive in a Fortune 500 company was the idea of success. Now in her mid-40s, she sees and understands that her original thoughts couldn't be further from the truth. She stated, "I was young and naive and thought money was everything, but enjoying what you do daily is the meaning of success to me." Other participants felt that training and assisting others fulfilled their idea of success in addition to the ability of able to apply what they have been taught and move up the ranks.

Research Question 4 Findings

Research question number 4 was aligned with participants' information, pertaining to the economic and social background influential factors they identified. Table 4 illustrated the cultural deficits, diversity/fairness, personal challenges and professional challenges aligned with this research question. The participant responses to this research question contributed greatly to the amount of information for this study.

Cultural Deficits Theme

Several theme codes evolved from the participant responses related to this theme. Themes of cultural deficits of African Americans and women, cultural differences and cultural idiosyncrasies appeared the most. Some participants indicated that people within similar or same cultures tend to have an easy time in developing relationships that lead to more opportunities or opportunities in general. The participants were intuitively cognizant of the fact that one must be a member of the dominant club socializing inside and outside of the workplace.

Forty percent of the participants mentioned that some of the relations and career advancement decisions occur outside the workplace. There were fervent conversations about not having an interest in doing the extracurricular type activities, such as playing tennis, having drinks or playing a round or two of golf whether they are having an after-work related activity such as birthday celebrations or a team meeting. The aforementioned forty percent stated that even though they are told not having an interest in doing extracurricular type activities is not an issue, they feel that they were being questioned and that others talked about them amongst other work-related groups in their respective organizations and outside the organizations. The forty percent also wondered whether non-participation in these activities is an important factor, and being African American women known for their resilience and ability to acclimate to any situation, should they conform or not conform. Each participant indicated that a positive African American woman cultural characteristic was the innate ability to juggle multiple priorities and work through challenges because they typically have these confrontations as part of their normal lives. Many attributed this cultural idiosyncrasy to how they were raised. Also, there was a common consensus that African American women are often seen as strong and or no-nonsense individuals. Consequently, these characteristics are sometimes evident when they become upset; this trait is sometimes not viewed as typical behavior.

102

Diversity and Fairness

Even though the glass ceiling has not been shattered, some believe that corporate culture has changed and improved; it is noted that there is definitely room for improvement. Some areas to improvement are diversity, mentoring, training and accountability. None of the participants believed that the glass ceiling has been broken, and 80 percent of the participants stated that they do not think that the glass ceiling will ever be shattered due to America still being dominated by White males, even with more emerging female leaders.

All of the participants are aware that America and the world in general is very diverse, especially with people coming from other nations into the United States within the past 10 years; hiring practices have changed; and some improvements have been made, but the glass ceiling still is prevalent. Some participants stated that their workplaces have diversity training along with workplace harassment training every other year, which may help management –especially new managers and leaders that come aboard. Some organizations are trying to change their mindset when it comes to diversity.

Personal Challenges

The most common personal challenge for the participants was balancing family and a career. The most difficult personal challenge for majority of the participants was the ability to balance work life and family life. One manager stated that many times she was faced with deciding whether to work later in order to sufficiently meet a deadline or to call it a day and go home and spend time with her family. This same participant also stated she has had to miss a few of her son's high basketball games and felt terrible about doing so.

Even though all of the participants discussed numerous personal and professional challenges, majority of them have found ways to conquer those challenges. African American women have faced many challenges throughout the years but have prevailed in the workplace and at home by turning their challenges into opportunities. Three participants stated that they regretted working additional hours with other state agencies or in the private sector instead of spending that additional time with their family.

Professional Challenges

The most common professional challenges amongst the participants were overcoming racism, stereotypes and negativity in the

104

workplace. The women all agreed at some point their professional careers that they have been faced with some sort of racism and stereotyping in the workplace. One participant stated that due to her very light-skinned complexion, a White male co-worker who is in management told her that she could pass for a White woman and would be able to "get away" with it and move up the ranks faster. The participant further stated, "I shouldn't be surprised, because I've told by black, white and Hispanics that I could pass for white all my life, but I was shocked that this co-worker of mine that I've known for over 15 years and worked directly with 8 of the 15 years would have let a statement of such be made to me. I couldn't say anything; I was too baffled to speak. All I could say to myself was, 'Damn, not you too!'"

Another participant stated that she was told by a white female manager that the only reason she got the job was to fulfill an equal opportunity quota and needed to hire a black female and she seemed to be the most qualified out of the bunch of blacks that applied and interviewed. The participant stated, "I felt like crap, I felt so small, like I was not worthy of having the position and the manager acted like I should be kissing her feet and singing her praises for my job." Another participant expressed that no matter how high they moved and climbed up the corporate ladder, African American women were still going to judged and not taken as sincerely as other races in the workplace. Also, for some individuals, in this day and age, it is still hard for them to accept blacks in management and be their manager."

All of the participants also felt that African American women should avoid negativity as much as possible. The participants felt like if African American women show the slightest sign of negativity in the workplace, the perceptions of what some people already have of African American will prevail. One participant felt like she was looked down on due to her coming from a poor household and did not have what some others growing up did. A White co-worker of hers went to the same high school, and she remembered how poor she was. The White co-worker even made a comment to her one day, saying, "You sure have come a long ways. I remember you were so poor, that I didn't think you would become who you are today." The participant then said she asked the co-worker what was meant by that statement. The co-worker then stated, "Well most people from your background never make anything of themselves. They're on welfare and/or on drugs, but you made it." The participant was floored by the co-worker's statement and surprised. "I shouldn't be surprised, but unfortunately that's how

106

many people view African Americans, based upon their backgrounds. Yes, I grew up a poor disadvantaged youth in New Jersey and North Carolina, but I was able to put myself through school and earn not one, but three degrees. It's truly sad that this co-worker's mindset is (similar to) the perceptions of so many others."

The advice that was given by the participants for other African American women is to always remain professional at all times, even when you do not want to and remember someone is always watching and scrutinizing you. There was also a common agreement between the participants that occasionally when individuals move up the ladder, stigmatisms and sometimes rumors follow those individuals to their new positions. The consensus from the participants was that individuals in the workplace is always looking at what you wear, what you say and how you say things and they observe the way that you think, which goes for other African Americans in the workplace, male and female. One participant stated one agency she worked for suffered from what she refers to as the "crab in the barrel" syndrome. She defined this syndrome as people that are the same race as you that pulls you down or try to pull you back down into the barrel while you try to climb out the barrel to reach success. The participant further stated, "It's sad that you have some of your own people that don't want to see you successful and/or become more successful than you."

There was another agreement among the participants that there are not a lot of opportunities for African Americans in North Carolina state government. Many participants stated that the opportunities that were available were given to whites or Asians (especially in the Informational Technology field, as 6 participants stated), and the opportunities that were available were given to friends or relatives who lacked the experiences and skill sets. Five participants stated that they had applied for jobs in other state agencies but did not get screened for an interview or they were screened for an interview, went to the interview and the position went to someone that they believed did not have the required skill set' it was not due to them bombing the interviews. One participant said that the hiring manger which conducted the interview personally called her at home and told her how well she did and she enjoyed speaking with her and hoped to speak to her again soon. The Participant further stated, "I thought that was a real good indicator that the job was mine, but I was wrong. Three days later, I received a rejection letter via e-mail that another candidate was selected for the position. I was embarrassed because this manager called my professional references and everything. I have no criminal background, and all of my performance ratings have been very good since I've been in state government, so I did not understand what happened. I called the hiring manager to see what happened and she stated the selected candidate was a "better fit" for their organization, whatever that means."

Another participant stated that she applied for 45 positions in state government in a year and a half and only has been on three interviews. The participant declared, "I felt I did very well on the three interviews I did go on, but did not get the jobs. Two of the positions I applied for went to friends of the hiring manager, and the other position was offered to someone that came from the private sector. I started to wonder because of my education and background: Were the hiring managers of these applied for positions intimidated by me? There were a couple of positions that I applied for and didn't get screened in that were re-posted, and this time I didn't put all of my education and kept everything else word for word. Guess what, I got called in for an interview for both positions, but I declined the interviews. I really wanted to say to the hiring manager and the individual that screened my app, 'Thanks for participating in my little experiment,' but I chose the higher road and I may be filing a grievance soon."

Another participant stated, "It's a shame that I and so many others cannot get screened in and or interviews for some of these positions. These same hiring managers (who are White) that won't screen us in and give us these interviews, call me and e-mail me on what to do in their organizations and ask me for my views and opinions on what to do, but won't give me an interview for nothing! It upsets me so, that I don't even want to come to work half the time any more. I get so disgruntled."

Chapter Summary

In synopsis, this chapter recapped the purpose of this research study and the particular research questions being focused on. This chapter also addressed and described the participants' backgrounds, demographic analysis and the significance of the participants' demographic information, and the researcher's data collection and methodologies. Lastly, this chapter offered outcomes based on the development of themes and theme codes and their corresponding alliance with the research questions.

Finally, the chapter closes by highlighting the individual responses of 18 African American women in management or leadership roles based on their own personal and professional experiences in North Carolina government in a White, male dominated culture. The study weighs today's evolution through this research and substantiates reliability of previous research findings through data analysis. Chapter 5 will present the study results, conclusions and recommendations; the researcher will provide recommendations for future areas of research.

CHAPTER FIVE: DISCUSSION, CONCLUSIONS AND RECOMMENDATIONS

Summary

In spite of the research efforts of theorists, feminists and women theologians, there is still an increasingly more diverse workforce than ever before. However, there is still an under-representation of African American women in management and leadership roles in organizations with White, male-dominated cultures. This study examined the perspectives of 18 African American women in North Carolina state government who are managers or leaders in three different North Carolina state governmental agencies. The participants' shared their individual perspectives on their journey on becoming a manger or a leader in their respective organizations, and their views were based on a personal and professional level and various influential factors such as race, gender, ethnicity, personal and professional challenges and leadership characteristics which is reflected in the data analysis.

This chapter presents a summary of the research results and is compared to results of preceding research studies of Parker (1997), Linehan and Scullion (2001), Thomas (2001), Combs (2003), King (2003), Anderson (2004) and Johnson (2006). An exploration of the data will support the researcher in corroborating that the results effectively address the research questions. Furthermore, this chapter introduces the African American women Model of Distinctiveness and Individualism.

The African American women Model of Distinctiveness and Individualism model cooperatively describes the establishment of 18 African American women's various endurance and the formation of their state of survival in the workplace facing the glass ceiling syndrome. The African American Women Model of Distinctiveness and Individualism demonstrates that redemption, lived experiences (personal and professional), perseverance and faith are the convictions which African American women stand.

Combs (2003) proposed that the dichotomy of race and gender might be driving African American women in managerial and leadership roles into an out-group status. An example of this out-group status is based on a statement from participant #4. The participant stated she has a female cousin that is in a leadership position in North Carolina state government that has her MBA from Duke University and a SPHR certification and was able to work her way up from being an office assistant to the role she has now, but her cousin lives an isolated life. The participant further stated, "Sometimes her cousin feels like she's walking on egg shells, she doesn't want to disrupt the flow of the office and make anyone upset. She just wants everyone to be happy and be happy with her, so she isolates herself to prevent any possible ill feelings towards her."

Butler and Skattebo (2004) theorized that society has stereotyped people by gender. In this theory, they indicated that society has identified certain races and gender and have given these individuals a title and a certain distinctive set of characteristics. One participant said, "Women are stereotyped in general, and when you add race and ethnicity to the equation, the situation can be compounded and difficult for some individuals to succeed in the work place." According to Johnson (2006), "Social role theorists and researchers explain that the basis for this stereotyping is because women are more likely than men to occupy roles that require communal qualities."

Summary of Theoretical and Research Findings

This section of the study addressed the summary of research findings as individual research questions. There is also an opportunity to associate outcomes of the exploration to a particular question. The use of specific participants 'quotes provide opportunities to correlate the responses to the research question.

African American women serving in leadership roles, such as in upper management in organizations? The results reveal that the characteristics of African American women in leadership roles, especially in upper management, are determination, dedication and faith. The women are teachers and each participant has a passion for teaching others so that they will not have to struggle as hard as they had to at the beginning of their careers.

Research question number 2 asked, "Is there a significant difference in the leadership behavior and style of African American women leaders versus White, Hispanic and Asian women and White, Hispanic and Asian males and what the differences if any are? The results revealed that there is not a major difference between White, Hispanic and Asian men and women. However, there are some differences between the four races identified in the study and the responses from all participants felt there are some similarities and differences. Parker, (1996) stated,

"One major gender leadership difference is that female leadership is relational and environmental, as opposed to male leadership which exhibits dictatorial and autocratic strategies.

Interestingly, black women exhibit both gender leadership

qualities, resulting in 'the cement wall,' in which they are black,

female, and exhibit direct male qualities."

African American women employees who elevate to the highest

positions in the workplace in the United States and the African

American women who do not receive advancements and what type of

relationship levels are there? The results showed that African American

women that hold a degree versus African -Americans that do not hold a

degree have a 90% chance in receiving and obtaining a higher position

in an organization than the individuals that do not have a degree, only a

high school diploma.

According to the Journal of Blacks in Higher Education (2010)

"African Americans that possess a four year college degree not only

greatly increases the incomes of African Americans but goes almost all

the way to close the economic gap between blacks and whites." (JBHE,

2010) also stated,

"Varying levels of education also makes a difference in pay

levels and advancements for African Americans, especially for

African American women. African Americans with a two-year

associate's degree improve their income by only 41 percent over blacks with just a high school diploma. However, African American women with a four-year college degree surpass African American women with a high school diploma by 99.5 percent. In 2003, African American women with only a high school diploma had a median income of $18,396. The median income of African American women with a bachelor's degree was $36,694."

Eight of the participants voiced a strong opinion that having a degree over just having a high school diploma is significant and by having a four year degree or advanced degree, the opportunity to move up the corporate ladder is greater. Participant #12, stated,

"When I first came to the agency, I didn't have a degree, just my high school diploma. I realized that the White women and White men as well as Asians were being looked at and promoted over me and others that did not have a degree. I decided from that day, I was going back to school, even if it killed me. Not only did I receive my B.S. in business, but I went on two years later and received my

MBA from University of Phoenix. I'm glad that I did receive the degrees, because I have received two promotions. My first promotion was within my first agency that I was employed with in

NC state government and recently another promotion to another

agency. I feel if I had not gone back to school, I would be

stuck in my old role and position."

The other 10 participants had mixed feelings about having a degree

over a high school diploma. Participant # 5 stated,

> "I have just my high school diploma and I've been a manger
>
> for 6 years and I have no desire to go back to school. I'll get
>
> certifications in different things, but no desire for a degree at
>
> this time in my life. Everything seems to be going OK   for
>
> me at work and home, so I'm good with that and where I am at
>
> this point in life. Now, would I like another job, absolutely,
>
> but for now, I'm ok."

The other participants felt that they do not necessarily think that higher

education will get you promoted and higher pay, it helps to have that

degree, but believes that experience holds more weight than the degree.

Question number 4 asked, "Does economic and social

background, such as coming from a poor, middle or upper class setting

play a deciding factor in an African American woman's ability to

obtain a leadership role in an organization? Results from this question

revealed that all 18 participants were in agreement that an individual's socio-economic background could play a role in an African American's ability to obtain a leadership role in an organization. Out of the 18 participants, 8 felt socio-economic played a significant role, while the 10 other participants felt socio-economic backgrounds does not play a significant role. King (1998) states, "It is mistakenly granted that either there is no difference in being black and female from being black (i.e., make) or generically female (i.e., white)." In Kings' findings she concluded that both institutionally and culturally that socio-economics play a significant role for African Americans in general but more so for African American women. Since the days of slavery, African American women have been stigmatized and ostracized for being who they are. King (2004) further stated,

"The group experience of slavery and lynching for blacks, genocide for Native Americans, and military conquest for Mexican-American and Puerto Ricans is not substantively comparable to the physical abuse, social discrimination, and cultural denigration suffered by women. No other group in America has so had their identity socialized out of existence as have black women."

In 1998, Helms, Fitzpatrick and Hwang concluded that "Attitudinal differences between middle- and lower-class blacks can be anticipated because they occupy different social and spatial locations in society and middle class African Americans are more supportive of the very system which they have benefited from." This viewpoint proposes, "That the same status differences that separate African Americans and Whites also separate middle- and lower-class blacks. As the socioeconomic disparity among black Americans broadens, so should their dissimilarities in insolences and world view."(Cuny.edu, 2009). In addition, the curtailing of status distance amongst middle-class African American and whites translates into social and spatial assimilation of the former. This study also concluded that middle class African Americans were more likely to assist one another when searching for jobs and homes, and White Americans were more willing to assist them because of their status versus lower class African Americans.

Theoretical and Research Findings

The conjectural and research findings from the selected academic sources discussed in the literature review chapter provide an all-inclusive understanding of the inimitable challenges of the treatment

120

and methods of endurance, leadership and managerial abilities for African American women. These theoretical findings and research are consistent with this study's finding in that society and social systems continue to operate covertly with subtle sexism and racism. After a review of past theoretical research and studies, current research findings, the analysis of this research study data, Theory of Self-Origination Distinctiveness emerged from this study.

This theory expands the work of Frances Ellen Watkins Harper, who increased and revised the work of Ralph Waldo's original notion of self-reliance in term of race, class, and gender (Hoeller, 2005). Mainly, the development pertains to increasing the concept of self-reliance to include self-origination. Development of this theory offers governmental leaders support in grasping the progressive behaviors and characteristics of African American women. Publication of this study offers processes that permit access to material pertaining to this theory.

The researcher through development of previous compositions of Harper's concept of self-reliance in terms of race, class, and gender (Hoeller, 2005), the researcher is able to illustrate an additional level of elements beyond the elements that Harper presents. This development enables the researcher to associate the additional level of components to the Theory of Self-Origination Distinctiveness, which particularly

focuses on African American women. Figure 1 illustrates the additional

level of elements interposing to Harper's work:

Figure 1

Expansion of Harper's Work

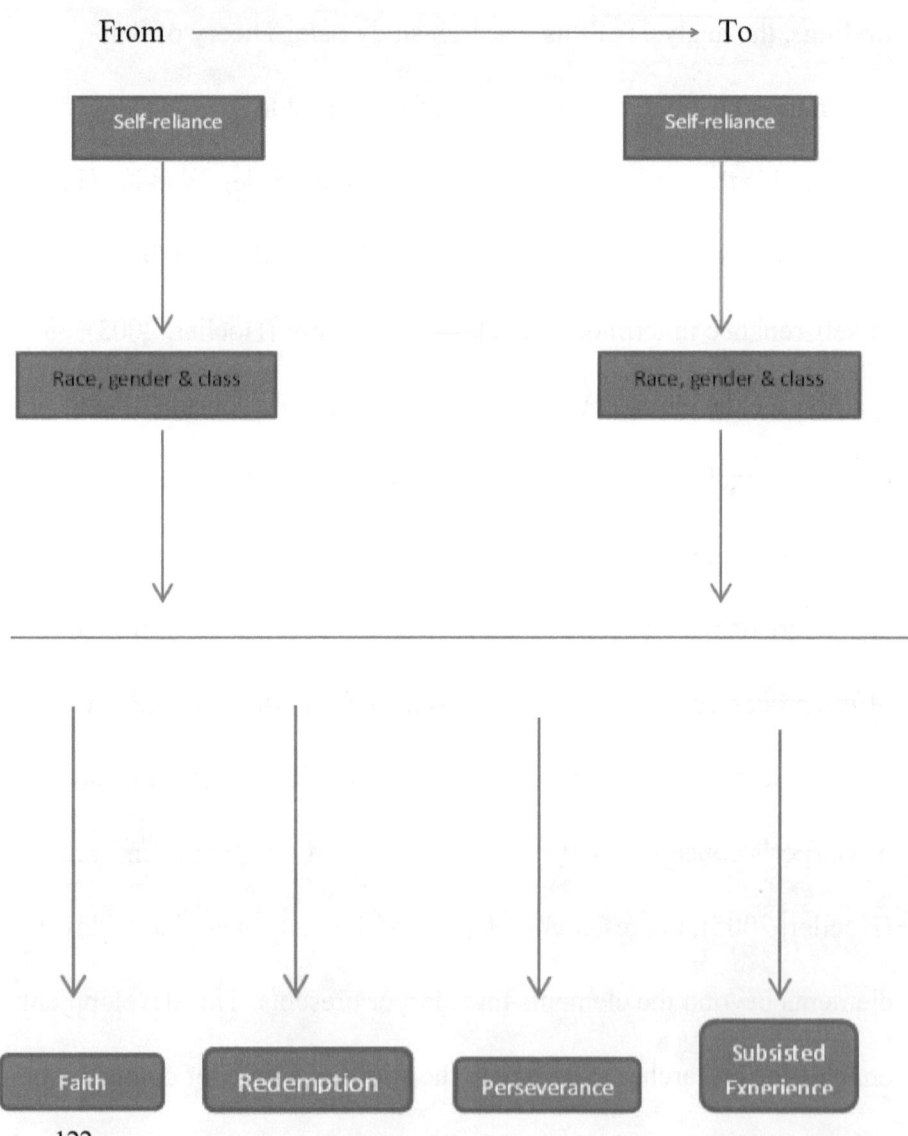

This study also captures the personal and professional experiences of 18 African American women, each of who communicate their methods in making choices pertaining to family and career. The participants' responses are harmonious with Thomas (2001) womanist theological perception of the capability of African American women to live assuredly within a culture of their own taking and devoid of concession of identity, faith and veracity.

For an example, participant #12 stated, "I feel that values are very important, especially since I'm a Christian. A Christian value-based system is meant to assist and not destroy." Another participant stated, "I try my best to avoid office politics, but sometimes I find myself getting roped into it. I hate when I do get caught up in office politics, then I find myself compromising my values and morals, then I feel bad."

Through the participants' responses, they speak vividly and candidly of maintaining their values and morals. The participants also indicated that whatever the personal or professional challenges may be, a woman should never negotiate her value system. The participants' responses supports Boas' (1999) proposal that theories of transformational leadership and charismatic leadership provide important insights as to the nature of effective leadership, especially because the emphasis is on emotions and values. This emphasis also supports past studies pertaining to leadership in several aspects ranging from emergence to styles and motivational factors (Bono & Judge, 2003); Chan, 2001).

Figure 2 introduces the new leadership model that emerged from this study and developed by the researcher, which grounds the profile of these 18 African American women.

Figure 2

African American Woman Model of Self-Origination

Distinctiveness

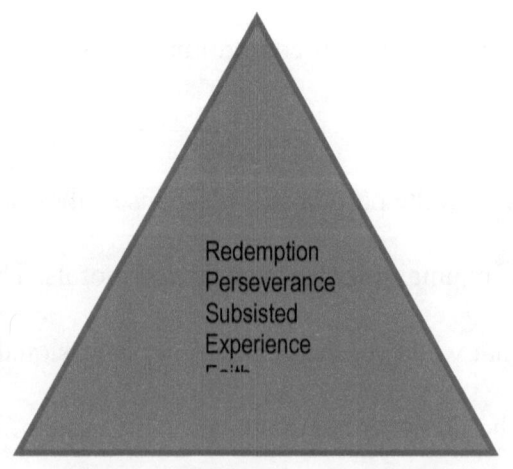

Redemption
Perseverance
Subsisted
Experience

In the canonical logic, redemption is the preservation from knowing obliteration or catastrophe. The redemption portion of the model for the 18 African American women, pinpoints how the participants have long endured on faith, a belief that is harmonious with the McManus and Roman's (2005) article, "Persons of Color and Religious at the Same Time: The Oblate Sisters of Providence, 1828-1860." The article pertains to the Oblate Sisters of Providence, founded in Baltimore in 1828, who were the first community of African American religious women in the United States.

McManus and Ronan's article is based on the sisters, who were free women of color. They developed, staffed and sustained the first schools in Baltimore for the education of free black children and created a religious institute that today continues their religious and ministerial vision. This article is faith based and suggests that African American women aspire to nurture, teach, and encourage which is consistent with the participants responses and each participant voiced that they were committed to mentoring and teaching others, especially women of color. As previously stated, the participants' voiced survival strategies for in and outside the workplace to bear their personal and professional challenges. Perseverance is the ability to tolerate adversity, hardship or strain. Earlier, Combs (2003) suggested that the duality of race and gender might be forcing African American women in managerial and leadership roles and positions into out-group status. Combs suggested that unconfirmed associations for African American women in leadership and managerial positions could be less affable and function under altered magnitudes than their White female counterparts. She further established that African American women totter an uncertain tightrope in the managerial field.

The Subsisted Experience section of the African American Woman Model of Self- Self-Origination Distinctiveness for the 18 African American women focuses on their survival and management of their personal and professional challenges pertaining to issues such as:

1. Always having opportunities
2. Avoiding relationships outside of work
3. Building an knowledge base
4. Completing undesirable tasks and duties from co-workers
5. Discussing issues or concerns competently
6. Domestic (family) support
7. Managing through personal and professional challenges
8. Not giving up

9. Prioritizing family

This material demonstrates the significance of family, fortitude and ability that the participants use to subsist and cope with their individual and professional lives and challenges.

The Faith section of the African American Woman Model of Self- Origination Distinctiveness focuses on the 18 African American women in management and leadership and their views and opinions on the world and how faith plays a role in their professional and personal lives. This study supports one of Thomas' (2000) objectives in that it explores the collective interpretation of the adult years in relation to their faith and society. For an example, a participant stated,

> " "I have much faith in my spirit, not just as a woman of color but as a human being. I believe that one's own values and principles that you live by in your personal life should be applied in the workplace that should be standard for everyone."

The model and theory are instruments to benchmark organizational leaders in grasping the culture of African American women. Publication of this inquiry study provides a means that permits access to data relating to these instruments. The African American

Woman Model of Self-Origination Distinctiveness is coherent with Thomas' (2002) womanist theology in that it amalgamates the necessary connection between these 18 African American women and the struggle, perseverance and faith of women of color in and separate of the workplace through the world by deliberately pursuing and engrossing the cultural perspectives of women who are part of the African ethos.

Conclusions

The intent of this research study was to understand the professional and personal experiences of African American women working in three North Carolina State governmental agencies in leadership and management. The sample population of 18 African American women limits generalization of the research findings and aims to understand the experiences of these women. Specifically, the sample population did not allow for generalization of the research data to represent African American women outside of 18 participants. This limitation is based on the following factors; the sample size is too small, the number of state agencies solicited for this study is too narrow; and organizational policies and procedures pertaining to diverse employees are vague. As a result, study conclusions are limited

128

to the 18 participants and generalizations beyond that will be formed in the mind of the reader.

The participants' responses indicate that race and gender continue to contribute to the low representation of African American women managers and leaders within their respective organizations. As discussed in Chapter 1, despite the research efforts of feminists, womanist theologians and theorists, there is an increasingly more diverse workforce and continues to be an issue with an inadequate representation of African American women in management and leadership roles and positions in organizations especially in the area of organizational leadership in a world of White, male-dominated cultures, the glass ceiling still exists (Votter, Hermsen, Ovadia & Vanneman, 2001). The participants' responses specify that factors such as lack of training, stereotyping, guidance, organizational structure, dealing with in effective supervisors and visibility continue to plague African American women within their respective organizations. As stated in Chapter 4, the majority of the participants believe that the glass ceiling still exists; they also acknowledge that things in the workplace are slowly showing signs of improvement; and there is still the necessity for additional progress.

This research study concludes that the 18 African American women participants often face challenges of fitting in with their peers in the workplace when advancing their careers. In addition, the implementation of many mentoring, diversity and affirmative action programs within the participants' respective organizations fail to address the underlying problems dealing with subtle diversity issues, such as racism and harassment in the workplace. These are still issues despite the participants' organizations holding programs such as violence in the workplace training and diversity effectiveness and initiatives programs (Eagly & Karau, 2002, Gilbert & Ivancevich, 2000; King, 2003; Jenkins, 2004; Lockwood, 2005).

Recommendations for Future Research

The researcher has four areas of suggested and recommended areas of research that derived from this study. The first proposed area for further doctoral research would be to develop this study over a period of time. The extension of this study will permit and offer an opportunity to continue following the 18 African American women's advancement in three to five years. Expansion of this research would facilitate the opportunity to further investigate the theory that developed from this study.

The second area for suggested future research is to survey the progression of African American women who are inclined to intermingle and be political in the workplace and build associations outside of work compared to White women. This suggested area of research is to study why civilization is still seeing more White women than African American women in managerial and leadership roles and positions and whether there it relates to their gender or race.

The third suggested area for future research would be to explore the attainment of conjugal interactions of African American women paralleled to White women as they progress into leadership and managerial positions and roles. This area of research suggests investigating if professional and personal encouragement makes a divergence in the marital relationships of African American women contrasted to their white counterparts.

In reviewing the research findings, the researcher advocates that the fourth area of suggested research should test the newly evolved model and theory, "The African American Woman Model of Self-Origination Distinctiveness" for cogency and dependability. Establishment of validity and reliability supports added leadership and management instruments for leaders concerning this theory and model. Hence, the researcher advocates additional research.

The researcher proposes that these fields be explored in more depth and detail for a few reasons; to establish if these instruments are successful and valuable for corporate, federal and state government agencies to use and implement in their workplaces, to establish if African American women use different subsistence methods from White women to cope and make selections, and to determine if the theory and model are able to facilitate to minimize the gap of the under-representation of African American women leaders and managers in non-profit and for profit organizations, therefore the researcher recommends further research.

REFERENCES

Ah Nee-Beham, M., & Cooper, J. (1998). *Let my spirit soar: Narratives of diverse women in school leadership.* Thousand Oaks, CA: Corwin.

Anderson, E. (2004). How not to criticize feminist epistemology: A review of Pinnick, Koertge and Almeder, scrutinizing feminist epistemology. Retrieved November 3, 2012 from http://plato.stanford.edu/entries/feminism-epistemology/

Argyris, C. (2000). *Flawed advice and the management trap.* New York, NY: Oxford University Press.

Austen, S., Jefferson, T. & Thein, V. (2003). Gendered social indicators and grounded theory. *Feminist Economics*, 9(1), 1-18.

Bass, B.M. (1985). *Leadership and performance beyond expectations.* New York: Free Press.

Baxter, E., Wright, J., & Birkelund, G (2000). The gender gap in

workplace authority: A cross national study. *American*

Sociological Review, 60(3), 401-435.

Beggs, J, .Villemez, W.J. and Arnold, R. 1997. Black population

concentration and black-white inequality: Expanding the

consideration of place and space effects. *Social Forces* 76:65-

91.

Bell, C. S. & Chase, S. E. (1993). Gender in the theory and practice of

educational leadership. *Journal for a Just and Caring*

Education 1, 200-222.

Bess, J.L. & Goldman, P. (2001). Leadership ambiguity in

universities and K-12 schools and the limits of contemporary

leadership theory. *The Leadership Quarterly 12*, 419-450.

Big Dog and Little Dog's Performance Juxtaposition. (1997, May 11

). *Concepts of leadership.* Retrieved August 27, 2012 from

http://www.nwlink.com/~donclark/leader/leadcon.html

Blalock, H. M. (1967). *Toward a theory of minority group relations.*

New York: Wiley.

Brunner, C. C. (1997). Working through the "middle of the heart": Perspectives of women superintendents. *Journal of School Leadership, 7*(3), 138-162.

Bureau of Labor Statistics (2002). Bureau of labor statistics census. Retrieved October 22, 2012 from http://www.bls.gov

Burr, J.A., O.R. Galle, and M.A. Fossett. (1991). Racial occupational inequality in Southern metropolitan areas: 1940-1980: Revisiting the visibility-discrimination hypothesis. *Social Forces* 69:831-50.

Butler, A.B. & Skattebo, A. (2004). What is acceptable for women may not be for men: The effect of family conflicts with work on job-performance rating. *Journal of Occupational and Organizational Psychology, 77*, 553-564.

Casmir, G. (2001). Combinative aspects of leadership style: The ordering and temporal spacing of leadership behaviors. *The Leadership Quarterly, 12*, 245-278.

Catalyst. (2004). Advancing *African American women in the workplace: Catalyst's new guide for managers.* Retrieved October 16, 2008 from http://www.catalystwomen.org

Coleman, M. (2005). Gender and secondary school leadership. Gender Issues in Leadership, 33(2), 3-19.

Collins, A. (2009, February 12). African American women face serious challenges in climb up the corporate ladder: the glass hammer. Retrieved from http://www.theglasshammer.com/news/2009/02/12/AfricanA merican-women-face-serious-challenges-in-climb-up-the-corporate-ladder/

Collins, P. H. (2000). *Black feminist thought: Knowledge, consciousness, and the politics of empowerment.* New York: Routledge.

Conger, J.A. & Kanungo, R. (1994). Charismatic leadership in organizations: Perceived behavioral attributes and their measurement. *Journal of Organizational Behavior, 15,* 439-452.

Cooper, D.R. & Schindler, P.S. (2003). Business research methods
(8th ed). Boston: McGraw-Hill Irwin.

Cotter, D., Hermsen, J., Ovadia, S., & Vannerman, R. (2001). The
glass ceiling effect. *Social Forces, 80*(2), 655-681.

Creswell, J. (1998). *Qualitative inquiry and research design:*
Choosing among five traditions. Thousand Oaks, CA: Sage
Publications.

Dardaine-Ragguet, P. (1994, January). Female administrators in urban
settings: Legal implications for policy and practice. Urban
Education, 28 (4), 398-411.

Eagly, A.H. & Johannesen-Schmidt, M.C. (2001). The leadership
styles of women and men. *Journal of Social Issues, 57*(4),
781-797.

Emerald Insight. (2004). Breaking the glass ceiling: *African American*
women in management positions. Retrieved January 31, 2012
from
http://www.emeraldinsight.com/journals.htm?articleid=88081
1&show=abstract&l ang=en_US&output=json&session-
id=d2d7e9f4fc262f361a5797fd7acdc31d

Federal Glass Ceiling Commission. (1992, 1995). *A solid investment: Making full use of the nation's human capital*. Washington: DC, U.S. Department of Labor.

Fossett, M.A., and Kiecolt, K.J.. (1989). The relative size of minority populations and white racial attitudes. *Social Science Quarterly* 70:820-35.

Fox-Keller, E., (1998). *Feminism and Science*. Oxford: Oxford University.

Glenn, Norval D. (1963). Occupational benefits to whites from the subordination of Negroes. *American Sociological Review* 28:443-48.

Gilligan, C. (1986). *In a different voice: Psychological theory and women's development.* Cambridge, MA: Harvard University Press.

Giscombe, K. & Matis, M.C. (2002). Leveling the playing field for women of color in corporate management: Is the business case enough? *Journal of Business Ethics,* 37(1), 103-119.

Goulding, C. (2003). Grounded theory: A magical formula or a potential nightmare. *The Marketing Review*, 2 (1), 21-34.

Grin (2010). A study of African American women: *The impact of the glass ceiling syndrome on advancement opportunities in organizations.* Retrieved September 18, 2012 from http://www.grin.com/en/doc/229049/a-study-of-African American-women-the-impact-of-the-glass-ceiling-syndrome?&lang=en_us&output=json&sessionid=052333bce 52a473cc001e8eeb0d19aec

Gyant, L. (1996). Passing the torch. *Journal of Black Studies, 26*(5), 629-648.

Hemmons, W. (1996). The African American Family and the US legal system. *Marriage and Family Review, 21*(3/4) 77-98.

Howard-Hamilton, M. (2003). Theoretical frameworks for African American women. *New Directions for Student Services, 104,* 19-28.

Huffman, M.L., and P.N. Cohen. (2004). Racial wage inequality: Job segregation and devaluation across U.S. labor markets. *American Journal of Sociology* 109 (4): 902-36.

Ivancevich, J.M. & Gilbert, J.A. (2000). Diversity management: Time for a new approach. *Public Personnel Management, 29* (1), 75-92.

Jacob, E. (1998). Clarifying quantitative research: A focus on

traditions. *Educational Researcher*, 17 (1), 16-24.

Jacobs, J.A. (1992). Women's entry into management—Trends in

earnings, authority and values among salaried managers.

Administrative Science Quarterly 37 (2): 282-301.

Jago, A. G. (1982). Leadership: Perspectives in theory and research.

Management Science, 28(3), 315-336.

Johnson, A.D. (2005). Which women of color earn the most? When

will they catch up to men? *DiversityInc.com.* Retreived October

22, 2012 from

http://www.diversityinc.com/members/6750print.cfn.

Johnson, P.R. (2010, May). Still missing in action: *The perceptions of*

African American women about the barriers and challenges

in ascending to the superintendency in North Carolina public

schools.

Jones, E.H., & Montenegro, X.P. (1982). *Recent trends in the*

representation of women and minorities in school

administration and problems in documentation. Arlington,

VA: American Association of School Administrators.

Kanter, R. M. 1977. *Men and women of the corporation.* New York: Basic Books. Key, J.P. (1997). Research design in occupational education. Retrieved January16, 2013 from: http://www.okstate.edu/ag/agedcm4h/academic/aged5980a/59 80/newpage21.htm

Kushner, K.E., & Morrow, R. (2003). Grounded theory, feminist theory, critical theory. *Advances in Nursing Science*, 26 (1), 30-43.

Lowe, K.B. & Gardner, W. L. (2001). Ten years of the leadership quarterly: Contributions and challenges for the future. *Leadership Quarterly, 11*(4), 459-   514.

Madame Noire. (2012, July 9). The big idea: 7 groundbreaking black female inventors. Retrieved August 30, 2012 from http://madamenoire.com/192852/the-big-idea-7-groundbreaking-black-female-inventors/#

Maxwell, J. (2005). *Qualitative research design: An interactive approach*. Thousand Oakes, CA: Sage Publications.

Merriam, S.B. (1998). *Qualitative research and case study applications in education.* San Francisco: Jossey-Bass.

Miller, S., Washington, Y., & Fiene, J.R. (2006). Female

    superintendents: Historic barriers and prospects for the future.

    Journal of Women in Educational Leadership, 4(4), 219-242.

Mittra, A. (2003). Breaking the glass ceiling: African American

    women in management positions. *Equal Opportunities*

    International, 22 (2), 67-79.

Mullings, L. (1997). *On our own terms: race, class and gender in the*

    lives of African American women. New York: Routledge.

Murtadha, K., & Larson, R. (1999, April). *Towards a socially critical,*

    womanist theory of leadership in urban schools. Paper

    presented at the annual meeting of the American Educational

    Research Association, Montreal, Canada.

Myers, M. (2000). Qualitative research and the generalizability

    question: Standing firm with proteus. *The Qualitative Report,*

    4(3/4) 127-138.

Northouse, G. (2007). Leadership theory and practice. (3rd ed.)

    Thousand Oak, London, New Delhe, Sage Publications,

Inc.O'Hare, P., Pollard, K., Mann, T., & Kent, M. (1992). African

    Americans in the 1990s. Population Bulletin, 46, 1.

Olzak, S., Shanahan, S. and West, E. (1994). School desegregation, interracial exposure, and antibusing activity in contemporary urban America. *American Journal of Sociology* 100:196-241.

Osuoha, R. (2010). *A study of African American women: The impact of the glass ceiling syndrome on advancement opportunities in organizations.* Retrieved August 27, 2012 from http://www.grin.com/en/doc/229049/a-study-of-African American-women-the-impact-of-the-glass-ceiling-syndrome

Parker, P.S. (2003). Learning leadership: communication, resistance and African american's women executive leadership development. Retrieved August 27, 2012 from http://www.cios.org/EJCPUBLIC/013/2/01326.html

Patterson, J.A. (1994, March). *Shattering the glass ceiling: Women in school administration.* Paper presented at the meeting of Women's Studies Graduate Symposium, University of North Carolina, Chapel Hill, NC.

Pfeffer, J. (1983). Organizational demography. In *Research in organizational behavior*, ed. Larry L.Cummings and Barry M. Staw, 299-359. Greenwich, CT: JAI.

Pfeffer, J., and Davis-Blake, A. (1987). The effect of the proportion of

women on salaries: The case of college administrators.

Administrative Science Quarterly 32:1-24.

Policy Almanac Org (2002). Federal anti-discrimination laws.

Retrieved September 14, 2012 from

http://www.policyalmanac.org/culture/archive/discrimination.sh

tml?&lang=en_us   &output=json&session-

id=ade8bdc4389a0aedbadbcac569bdb150

Porter, J. (2002). An investigation of the glass ceiling in corporate

America: *The perspective of African American women.*

Dissertation Abstracts International, 64 (01). (UMI No.

3078972)

Quillian, L. (1996). Group threat and regional change in attitudes

toward African Americans. *American Journal of Sociology*

102:816-60.

Redwood, R. (1996). The glass ceiling: the findings and

recommendations of the federal glass ceiling commission.

Retrieved December 6, 2012 from

http://www.inmotionmagazine.com/glass.html

Reskin, B.F., and D.B. McBrier. (2000). Why not ascription?

    Organizations' employment of male and female managers.

    American Sociological Review 65 (2): 210-33. 3078972)

Robson, C. (2002). Real world research: *A resource for social*

    scientists and practitioner researchers (2nd ed). Malden, MA:

    Blackwell Publishing.

Rusher, A.W. (1996). *Black women administrators*. Lanham, MD:

    University Press of America.

Seidman, I.E. (1991). *Interviewing as Qualitative Research.* New

    York: Teachers College Press.

Smith, A.M. (2008). Race and gender on the leadership experiences

    of three female African American high school principals: a

    multiple case study. Retrieved August 27, 2012 from

    http://www.georgiasouthern.edu/etd/archive/fall2008/angela_d

    mosley/smith_angela_m_200808_edd.pdf

Smith, J. (1983). Quantitative versus qualitative research: An attempt

    to clarify the issue. *Educational Researcher*, 12(3), 6-13.

Stainback, Kevin, and Donald Tomaskovic-Devey. (2006). Managing

    privilege: The stable advantage of white males in U.S. labor

    markets, 1966-2000. Manuscript, University of

    Massachusetts, Amherst.

Tannen, D. (1994). *Talking from 9 to 5: Woman and men in the*

    workplace: Language, sex and power. New York: Avon.

Taylor, M.C. (1998). How white attitudes vary with the racial

    composition of local populations: Numbers count. *American*

    Sociological Review 63 (4): 512-35.

Thomas, L. E. (2000). Womanist theology, epistemology, and a new

    anthropological paradigm. *Cross Currents.* Retreived

    November 1, 2012 from http://www.aril.org/thomas.htm

University of Chapel Hill-North Carolina (2007, January). *Black*

    under-representation in management across u.s. labor

    markets. Retrieved January 31, 2013 from

    http://www.unc.edu/~pnc/AAAPSS07.pdf?&lang=en_US&out

    put=json&session-id=d2d7e9f4fc262f361a5797fd7acdc31d

Valverde, L. A. (2003). Influences on leadership development of

    racial and ethnic minorities. New York: Longman.

Yoder, J.D. (2001). Making leadership work more effectively for

women. *Journal of Social Issues, 57* (4), 815-828.

http://diversityessentials.wordpress.com/2008/10/15/African

American-female-leadership-styles/

http://www.jbhe.com/news_views/47_fouryear_collegedegree

s.htmlhttp://www.jstor.org/discover/10.2307/3174661?uid=37

39776&uid=2134&uid=2474554373&uid=2&uid=70&uid=3

&uid=3739256&uid=60&uid=2474554363&purchasetype=art

icle&accessType=none&sid=21102692092833&showMyJstor

Pss=false&seq=5&showAccess=false

http://maxweber.hunter.cuny.edu/pub/eres/SOC217_PIMENT

EL/hwang.pdf

APPENDICES

APPENDIX A

Interview Guide

1. How long have you been in your current position? What brought you to your agency?

2. What are your duties at your current agency, and did you perform the same duties at a past job?

3. How long have you been in your current field? What influenced you to enter into this type of field?

4. Was this your chosen career path, and if not, what was it?

5. What are some important factors you feel African American women should take into consideration when they're in management/leadership?

6. Did you know you wanted to be a manager/leader, and if yes, what was it that made you decide you wanted to be in management/leadership?

7. What value, if any, does your educational background add to your current position?

8. Describe to me in detail on how you got to where you are in your career.

9. Do you see yourself as successful, and what is your definition of being successful?

10. What contributed to your success in the workplace?

11. Have you always worked in the public sector, and if so, what made you work only in the public sector? If you have worked in the

private sector, please describe your job and duties in the private sector.

12. What are your management/leadership style and management/leadership characteristics?

13. What obstacles if any, did you have to overcome to get where you are currently in your career?

14. What were the most difficult barriers you faced on your way up the corporate ladder?

15. Have you ever been questioned on your abilities and skills of being an effective manager/leader?

16. Do you feel that you're treated differently being an African American woman in management/leadership than that of an African American male or other counterparts, such as white women or men, that are in the same position as you in the workplace?

17. Do you have any particular experiences you would like to share on a personal level regarding being a manager/leader?

18. Do you think that African American women are stereotyped in the workplace, and do these stereotypes hinder an African American woman from moving up the ranks in the workplace?

19. In your opinion, has the glass ceiling been shattered or does it still remain?

20. Do you feel you were properly trained to do your job, and if not, what are the areas you would like to be trained in?

21. Do you feel your workplace is culturally diverse? Be specific.

22. Do you know of any cultural differences that may play an important role in attaining management/leadership status?

23. When was your last promotion, and did you receive an increase in pay? If you received a promotional pay increase, do you feel the promotional pay increase was sufficient? If you did not receive an increase in pay, were you given a reason for not receiving a promotional increase and do you mind sharing the reason?

24. What advice or suggestions would you have for other African American women in management/leadership or those women seeking management/leadership positions?

25. Is there anything else you would like to add, or any comments you would like to add outside of the scope of these questions?

APPENDIX B

Participant Form

April 22, 2013

Dear _____,

You are cordially invited to participate in a research study. The purpose of this research study is to survey the views and opinions of African American women who are or has been in a managerial, leadership and or supervisory role(s) and to grasp a better understanding of African American women in these roles. You were chosen for this study based on data obtained through the state of North Carolina governmental employee data base and you met the research criteria for the study (see the attachment of qualifying criteria). If you participate in this research, you will be asked to take part of an interview process that will be 30 to 45 minutes.

The interview questions are based on your educational background, supervisory and leadership experience and to describe in your own view and opinion being an African American woman in the workplace and your roles and duties in the workplace. The interview will take place away from your work environment in order not to distract from your work related duties. A neutral location will be chosen so not to conflict with work related duties. Your real name will not be used in the study, but your name will be represented with a number (example: Participant 1, 4, 8, etc.) and your views and opinions will not be disclosed to others not associated with the research project (family members, other organizations) without your consent. The time and date of the interview will be determined once all University approvals have been received as well as your schedule and a follow up with to schedule the interview will take place via E-mail and or by phone.

Your participation in this research is strictly voluntary. You may refuse to participate at all, or choose to stop your participation at any point in the research, without fear of penalty or negative consequences of any kind.

The information/data you provide for this research will be treated confidentially, and all raw data will be kept in a secured file by the principal investigator. Results of the research will be reported as aggregate summary data only, and no individually identifiable information will be presented. The study will not cause any defamation of your agency and or your immediate work environment.

You also have the right to review the results of the research if you wish to do so. A copy of the results may be obtained by contacting the principal investigator at the e-mail, address or phone number below:

Natalie Montague
3816 Poulnot Ct
Raleigh, NC 27604
919.457.3916 or 347.480.8603
nmontague3@aol.com

There will be no monetary compensation provided to you as a participant; however, the results of the research may contribute to the business and business psychology fields, the profession, or to society as a whole.

Please do not hesitate to contact me if you have any additional questions, comments or concerns. Thank you for your support and participation in this study.

Sincerely,

Natalie A. Montague
Doctoral Candidate

Attachment(s): 1

APPENDIX C

Research Criteria for Study Participants

1. Participant must have had two years or more of management experience either in private or public sector and has applied and or interviewed for a higher position in management within the past 5 years.

2. Participant must be employed with the North Carolina state government for two years.

3. Education of any level which includes high school or college (individuals that attended college will not have to have a degree).

4. All sociocultural backgrounds (societal norms may vary for each participant)

5. All economic backgrounds accepted (poor, middle and upper class economic background of each participant).

6. Additional training or certifications received within the past 5 years.

7. Must be an African American Woman between the ages of 25 and 65.